An Introduction to the Biblical Worldview and Contemporary Moral Issues

RLGN 105

Rob Van Engen
Liberty University

TABLE OF CONTENTS

Becoming a Critical Thinker

Developing a Biblical/Christian Worldview

Contemporary Religious Worldviews

Tolerance and the Biblical/Christian Worldview

Biblical Worldview Application

CRITICAL THINKING
CHAPTER 1

What INFLUENCES the way we think?

-
-
-
-

BIBLICAL INSIGHT

Genesis 1-2 (NIV) - (especially 2:18 & 20) The LORD God said, "It is not good for the man to be alone. I will make a helper suitable for him." But for Adam no suitable helper was found.

- **1:26** **Let us make…**
- **2:18** **It is not good for man to be alone…**
- **2:20** **but Adam had no one like himself as a help.**

God is the _____ Critical Thinker!

Genesis 2:15-17 The Lord God took the man and put him in the Garden of Eden to work it and take care of it. And the Lord God commanded the man, "You are free to eat from any tree in the garden; but you must not eat from the tree of the knowledge of good and evil, for when you eat from it you will certainly die."

Genesis 2:19 whatever the man called each living creature, that was its name.

Genesis 3:1-7 An Encounter with a "crafty creature."

God is the Ultimate Critical Thinker

who taught _____ to be Critical Thinkers!

Proverbs 14:15 (NIV) - A simple man believes anything but a prudent man gives thoughts to his steps.

Colossians 2:8 (NLT) - Don't let anyone lead you astray with empty philosophy and high-sounding nonsense that come from human thinking and from the evil powers of this world, and not from Christ.

2 Corinthians 10:4-5 (NIV) - The weapons we fight with are not the weapons of the world. On the contrary, they have divine power to demolish strongholds. We demolish arguments and every pretension that sets itself up against the knowledge of God, and we take captive every thought to make it obedient to Christ.

Romans 12:2 (CEV) - Don't be like the people of this world, but let God change the way you think. Then you will know how to do everything that is good and pleasing to him.

1 Peter 3:15 (NIV) - But in your hearts set apart Christ as Lord. Always be prepared to give an answer to everyone who asks you to give the reason for the hope that you have. But do this with gentleness and respect

DEFINITION

1. It is recognizing and evaluating _____ and so-called _____.

2. It is reflecting on the meaning and significance of statements and _____.

3. It tests the _____ of statements and ideas.

CHARACTERISTICS

1. They constantly evaluate their own _____, _____ & _____.

2. They understand that having a _____ to an opinion does not mean that every opinion is _____, including their own.

3. They do not pretend to know what they do not know.

4. They do not blindly adhere to _____.

5. They resist and refuse to use _____.

6. They seek _____ of terms.

7. They explore the many sides of an issue.

8. They base their opinions and judgments on _____.

9. They are eager to learn from the experiences of others.

10. They look for _____ in the arguments of others.

TERMS

A. _____

Belief or conclusions about reality. Unlike facts, they are open to question and analysis by critical thinking.

B. _____

In the formal sense, it is an attempt to offer evidence to demonstrate the reasonableness of an opinion. Arguments can be sound (logical) or unsound (dependent upon logical fallacies).

C. The LAW OF NON-CONTRADICTION

> **"An idea cannot be both true and false at the same time in the same way."**

HISTORY

ARISTOTLE'S INSTRUCTION

It is impossible that the same thing belong and not belong to the same thing at the same time and in the same respect." (1005b19-20)

No one can believe that the same thing can (at the same time) be and not be." (1005b23-24)

The most certain of all basic principles is that contradictory propositions are not true simultaneously." (1011b13-14)

✓ Buddhism contains a philosophy called *Catuskoti* that rejects the law of non-contradiction.
http://en.wikipedia.org/wiki/Law_of_ non-contradiction

✓ Hinduism is a pluralistic religion (claims all religions lead to God) by nature. The fundamental tenet of Hinduism (all religions lead to God) violates the law of non-contradiction.
http://www.project315.net/hinduism-truth-test.html

✓ Islam, as you know, is very clearly an exclusive claim to God. A Muslim will never tell you that it doesn't matter what you believe or that all religions are true.

Ravi Zacharias (June 27, 2012)

D. LOGICAL FALLACIES

In rhetoric, a fallacy is simply any error, whether intentional or unintentional, in reasoning.

(The most common kinds of fallacies of logic are informal, and are the ones students really need to familiarize themselves with. Think of them as the **counterfeits** of arguments.)

1. _____ **Concluding that an effect has only one cause when it is really the result of multiple causes.**

Examples:
School violence has gone up and academic performance has gone down ever since organized prayer was banned at public schools. Therefore, prayer should be reintroduced, resulting in school improvement.

2. _____ _____ Making a judgment on the basis of one or even a few samples.

   Examples:
   "I loved the hit song, therefore I'll love the album it's on"
   False because the album might have one good song and lots of filler

3. _____ (Stereotyping) Making a judgment about an entire Group based on behavior, mostly undesirable, of a few from that group.

   Examples:
   I am at Liberty University where all students are Christians.
   All lawyers are unethical

4. _____ _____ Arguing on the basis of a comparison of unrelated things.

   Examples:
   Employees are like nails. Just as nails must be hit in the head in order to make them work, so must employees.
   People are like dogs. They respond best to clear discipline.
   This soap is like a dream. It lifts you up to a spiritual plane.

5. _____ _____ Arguing against an action on the unsupported assertion that it will inevitably lead to a much worse condition.

   Examples:
   "We have to stop the tuition increase! The next thing you know, they'll be charging $40,000 a semester!"
   Once all gun-owners have registered their firearms, the government will know exactly from whom to confiscate them.

6. _____ _____ Stating a general principle and then applying it in a specific case as though it were a universal rule.

   Examples:
   If he can lose weight, then you can too.
   If I can teach this class then so can anyone else.

7. _____ (Lit. "To the man") Seeking to discredit a person's argument by attacking their personal character, origin, associations, etc.

   Examples:
   Bill: I believe that abortion is morally wrong.
   Dave: Of course you would say that, you're a priest."
   Bill: What about the arguments I gave to support my position?
   Dave: Those don't count. Like I said, you're a priest, so you have to say that abortion is wrong. Further, you are just a lackey to the Pope, so I can't believe what you say.

8. _____ _____ _____ _____ **Appealing to the opinion of a person who agrees with yours because they are generally respected by the audience, but have no real authority on the topic at hand.**

Examples:

You shouldn't speak until you know what you're talking about. That's why I get uncomfortable with interviews. Reporters ask me what I feel China should do about Tibet. Who cares what I think China should do? They hand me a script. I'm a grown man who puts on makeup. *Brad Pitt*

9. _____ _____ _____ **Claiming that something is true simply because it cannot be disproved, or that something is untrue because it cannot be proved.**

Examples:

No one has ever proved that the Loch Ness Monster exists, so it must not exist.
No one has ever proved that the Loch Ness Monster does not exist, so it must exist.
You cannot prove that God does not exist, so He does.
You cannot prove that God exists, therefore He doesn't.

10. _____ **Justifying a course of action because "everyone is doing it."**

Examples:

Everyone is a Republican or Democrat so I should be also.
Bill: I like classical music and I think it is of higher quality than most modern music.
Jill: That stuff is for old people.
Dave: Yeah, only real woosies listen to that crap. Besides, Anthrax rules! It Rules!
Bill: "Well, I don't really like it that much. Anthrax is much better."

11. _____ / _____ ; **(naturalistic fallacy) Concluding about the way things ought to be simply on the basis of how things are or are assumed to be.**

Examples:

According to the Theory of Evolution, the best creatures will survive. Therefore we shouldn't make special efforts to feed the poor. If they can't survive on their own, that just means they aren't as good as we are.

12. _____ _____ **Looking only for things that support our current ideas, and ignoring evidence that does not.**

Examples:

I can say that I believe abortion is right because I have heard of a case in which it saved the life of the mother. In doing so, I totally overlook or ignore all the rest of the evidence

13. _____ _____ **Oversimplifying a complex issue to make it appear that only two alternatives are possible. (Either/Or fallacy)**

   Examples:
   Either 1+1=3 or 1+1=4
   Shape up or ship out
   We should either pay our teachers better salaries or admit that we do not care about our children's education.

14. _____ _____ **Raising an irrelevant issue to divert attention from the primary issue. Make appeals to fear and pity.**

   Examples:
   Smoke screen, wild goose chase
   Yes, my grades are low, but I do volunteer a lot of my time to help others.

15. _____ _____ **Ignores a person's actual position and substitutes a distorted, exaggerated or misrepresented version of that position.**

   Examples:
   The senator says we should not fund the attack submarine program. I disagree entirely. I can't understand why he wants to leave us defenseless like that.

IDENTIFYING LOGICAL FALLACIES
(PRACTICE)

(For practice, identify the fallacies. The answers follow the last example.)

1. Argument

"We need to round up every single person of Middle Eastern descent and ship them all back to their own country. If we are going to restore any sense of security to this great land, we need to take drastic measures and get rid of all these terrorists . . . and anyone who looks like one."

Fallacy: _____

2. Argument

"Everyone ought to be drinking Green Tea. The Chinese drink it all the time and they do not have near the incidents of heart disease that we do in the U.S. Further, most Chinese men live at least twenty more years than the average American male."

Fallacy: _____

3. Argument

"Here is my opponent, speaking to you of the values of abstinence and abstinence education when everyone knows she had a child out of wedlock while a teenager herself!"

Fallacy: _____

4. Argument

"The holocaust was a terrible misfortune, but while 6,000,000 Jews were killed during the Holocaust, there are over 600 million chickens killed every year just to satisfy our hunger for flesh!"

Fallacy: _____

5. Argument

"Hanes must be the best underwear on the market; you know they're Michael Jordan's favorites."

Fallacy: _____

6. Argument

"I know that God exists because no atheist, no matter how clever, has ever provided evidence to the contrary."

Fallacy: _____

7. Argument

"I cannot believe that the US, as civilized as it is, still allows the death penalty. Most other countries have already made capital punishment unlawful. How can the U.S. continue this barbaric practice?"

Fallacy: _____

8. Argument

"Because humans can be shown to do everything, ultimately, for their own benefit, we should always, and only, do that which is in our best interest."

Fallacy: _____

9. Argument

Person A: It has not been proven that the unborn are not persons, so shouldn't we err on the side of life? Has it never occurred that we just may be sanctioning murder?

Person B: Well, speaking of death, if, as my opponent desires, abortions were 'illegal except to save the woman's life', women will resort to "back-alley" abortions again, which are very unsafe and often deadly.

Fallacy: _____

10. Argument

"Did you see that child sipping wine? I can't believe her parents allow this. Today it's a few sips of wine; in ten years it's another problem alcoholic, driving drunk on the road, killing our loved ones!"

Fallacy: _____

11. Argument

"Gay rights are the issue of greatest importance at this time in our nation. It's the last oppression. The US must take this step in ending oppression, just like it did when it outlawed slavery and established civil rights for its black citizens."

Fallacy: _____

12. Argument

"Affirmative action means one thing: injustice. As we continue to set quotas that keep qualified white males from getting jobs, we are promoting reverse discrimination. Face it: if you are not against affirmative action, you are for injustice."

Fallacy: _____

13. Argument

"She will never make it in college. She made Cs and Ds in high school"

Fallacy: _____

14. Argument

"As Americans we believe in 'freedom of the press'; therefore, reporters should not be hindered from reporting our troops movements in the war zone."

Fallacy: _____

15. Argument

Bill and Jill are arguing about cleaning out their closets:

Jill: "We should clean out the closets. They are getting a bit messy."

Bill: "Why, we just went through those closets last year. Do we have to clean them out every day?"

Jill: "I never said anything about cleaning them out every day. You just want to keep all your junk forever, which is just ridiculous."

Fallacy: _____

ANSWERS:

1) Overgeneralization/Stereotyping

2) Oversimplification

3) Ad Hominen

4) False Analogy

5) Appeal to False Authority

6) Appeal to Ignorance

7) Bandwagon

8) Is/Ought - Naturalistic Fallacy

9) Red Herring

10) Slippery Slope

11) False Analogy

12) False Dilemma

13) Hasty Conclusion

14) Sweeping Generalization

15) Straw Man

UNDERSTANDING WORLDVIEW

CHAPTER 2

Worldview

NOT

merely our _____ of the world.

"Our society is really sinful."

NOT

limited to those who study _____.

Worldview

DEFINITION

world·view (wûrld′vyo͞o′) *n.* translated from German: **Weltanschauung.**

1. The overall perspective from which one sees and interprets the world.
2. A collection of beliefs about life and the universe held by an individual or a group.

**The American Heritage® Dictionary of the English Language,
Fourth Edition copyright ©2000 by Houghton Mifflin Company:**

WORLDVIEW IS...

Every worldview has a _____ **point.**

Every worldview makes _____ **(called presuppositions).**

A _____ **of life.**

The basis for moral _____ _____.

Simply put:

A Worldview is…

- **It is like looking through _____ glasses that affect everything we see.**

- **It is a basic set of _____ and assumptions about the most important things in life, like God, self, morality, truth, and the afterlife.**

- **People do not seriously think about their worldview until a _____ causes them to question life."**

LIST EXTERNAL FORCES THAT COULD INFLUENCE OUR WORLDVIEW:

- _____
- _____
- _____

- _____
- _____
- _____

WORLDVIEW ANSWERS...

The question of _____ (beginning)

How did life begin in the first place? Where did I come from?

The question of _____ (being)

What does it mean to be a human? Am I more important than animals?

The question of _____ (purpose)

Why are we here? Why am I here?

The question of _____ (ethics)

What is meant by right and wrong? How should I live?

The question of _____ (future)

Is there life after death? What will happen to me when I die? Will I have to answer for the choices I made and how I lived my life?

VALID WORLDVIEW

The standard for determining a valid worldview:

Must be _____ **My answers to the above questions must be consistent with one another; i.e. they must not contradict each other.**

Example: *The questions of origin and identity.*

Must be _____
My answers must deal truthfully and completely with all the facts it encounters.

Example: *Anthropic principle.*

1. conditions that are observed in the universe must allow the observer to exist—called also *weak anthropic principle*

2. the universe must have properties that make inevitable the existence of intelligent life —called also *strong anthropic principle*

Must be _____
My worldview must make sense of the emotions and feelings I have as I interact with the world around me.

Example: Why do I feel guilt, sadness, joy, etc.?

HISTORY

ANTHROPIC PRINCIPLE

The phrase "anthropic principle" first appeared in Brandon Carter's contribution to a 1973 Kraków symposium honoring Copernicus's 500th birthday. Carter, a theoretical astrophysicist, articulated the Anthropic Principle in reaction to the Copernican Principle, which states that humans do not occupy a privileged position in the Universe. As Carter said: "Although our situation is not necessarily central, it is inevitably privileged to some extent."

COMPETING WORLDVIEWS

_____ **The only reality exists in the natural realm.**

Examples: Secular Humanism - Man is the central focus of decision making.
Atheism - God does not exist. He is irrelevant.
Evolutionary change is inevitable.

_____ **God and the world are the same thing.**

Examples: Eastern religions, Christian Science, the New Age movement, etc.

_____ **God is the creator of the world and does not or cannot interfere with human-kind. Miracles do not exist.**

Example: Thomas Jefferson (?)

> ### INFORMATION
>
> God is identified through nature and reason, not revelation. Deists who believe in God, or at least a divine principle, follow few if any of the other tenets and practices of Christianity, Judaism, or any religion believing in a personal God. Any deist god is an eternal entity whose power is equal to his/her will.
>
> Deism has no need for ministers, priests, or rabbis. All an individual requires is their own common sense and the ability to contemplate their human condition.
> *www.allaboutphilosophy.org/deism.htm*

_____ **God exists, was the creator of the world, and is personally and intimately involved with His creation. God operates through natural law but can and does intervene in the affairs of humankind.**

Examples: Christianity, Judaism, and Islam

CONTEMPORARY AMERICAN SECULAR WORLDVIEW

The core of the modern western secular worldview is: materialism, subjectivism, hedonism, pragmatism, and postmodernism. Self has become the god of this worldview. Self has become the center of existence in this worldview.

1. _____

Philosophical concept: A society devoid of absolute Truth, and no spiritual anchor.

Social application: Seeking satisfaction and meaning in possessions. *What matters most is what you can see and touch.*

How is this seen in contemporary society?

2. _____

Philosophical concept: There is no absolute Truth.

Social application: "*Everyone is entitled to his/her opinion.*" Feelings become authoritative! Moral and social chaos ensues, for there are no absolutes of right and wrong. Moral judgments are based on your feelings. What may be true for you may not be true for me.

How is this seen in contemporary society?

3. _____

Philosophical concept: Defines pleasure and pain according to the human condition and sensory input alone. No other measure of good and evil.

Social application: Pursuit of pleasure, comfort, safety and security in human terms. All struggle and pain is defined as evil. Delayed gratification is considered to be evil. "If it feels good, do it!" Whatever causes pleasure is right for you.

How is this seen in contemporary society?

4. _____

Philosophical concept: A utilitarian philosophical belief that the end justifies the means.

Social application: The end justifies the means. Focus upon intentions rather than upon right and wrong. If "intentions" are good, it does not matter if what we are doing is wrong, according to this viewpoint. "Does it work?"
How is this seen in contemporary society?

5. _____

> *Philosophical concept*: Truth does not exist. Truth is whatever we can get our community to agree to. If we can get it to use our language, then our story is as true as any story will ever get.

> *Social application*: Those who have power (or the most influence) make the rules.

> *The facts of the story don't matter. No story can have any more credibility than any other story. All stories are equally valid and we can create our own stories.*
> **James Sire, The Universe Next Door InterVarsity Press, 1997**

How is this seen in contemporary society?

Genesis 1:1 (KJV) - In the beginning God created the heaven and the earth.

Job 14:14 (NIV) - If a man dies, will he live again? All the days of my hard service I will wait for my renewal to come.

Romans 12:1-2 (NLT) - And so, dear brothers and sisters, I plead with you to give your bodies to God. Let them be a living and holy sacrifice--the kind he will accept. When you think of what he has done for you, is this too much to ask? Don't copy the behavior and customs of this world, but let God transform you into a new person by changing the way you think. Then you will know what God wants you to do, and you will know how good and pleasing and perfect his will really is.

Acts 28:1-6 - Notice the reaction of the people based upon their worldview.

A BIBLICAL WORLDVIEW

Starts with… _____ (Genesis 1:1)

…who has chosen to reveal _____ (Hebrews 1:1-2)

How did God reveal Himself?

- _____ (Genesis 1:1)

- _____ (2 Timothy 3:16; 2 Peter 1:20-21)

The Bible is God's _____

- In human _____ (John 1:1-14; John 3:16)

The **Greatest Possible Being** (GPB) is _____.

What can be learned about GPB?

- _____

- _____

- _____

The Framework

C_____

F_____

R_____

> ## QUOTATION
>
> Worldview is an articulation of the basic beliefs embedded in a shared grand story that are rooted in a faith commitment and that give shape and direction to the whole of our individual and corporate lives.
> *Goheen, M. W. & Bartholomew, C. G. (2009). Living at the crossroads: An introduction to Christian worldview (p. 23).*

BIBLICAL WORLDVIEW IMPORTANCE

1. A worldview helps us integrate biblical principles with _____ (*glasses, lens, filter, mental map*).

2. A clear understanding of the biblical worldview provides _____ for and gives substance to our faith. (Luke 6:46-49).

3. A clear understanding of our worldview is essential because of an overt _____ from the secular world. (Ephesians 4:14).

4. A coherent worldview gives us a more effective _____ in the marketplace. (1 Peter 3:15).

5. A clear understanding of the Christian worldview is essential because the _____ has become our _____. (Titus 1:9).

6. We must clearly understand the Christian worldview because it is commanded in Scripture. (Colossians 2:6-7).

Making Sense of Your World Ken Hemphill, Lifeway Press, 1993

WORLDVIEW THOUGHTS

I am convinced that the battle for humankind's future must be waged and won in the public school classroom by teachers who correctly perceive their role as the proselytizers of a new faith: a religion of humanity that recognizes and respects the spark of what theologians call divinity in every human being. These teachers must embody the same selfless dedication as the most rabid fundamentalist preachers, for they will be ministers of another sort, utilizing a classroom instead of a pulpit to convey humanist values in whatever subject they teach, regardless of the educational level-- preschool day care or large state university. The classroom must and will become an arena of conflict between the old and the new-- the rotting corpse of Christianity, together with all its adjacent evils and misery, and the new faith of humanism.

John Dunphy, A Religion for a New Age, Humanist, Jan.-Feb. 1983

"Thinking Christianly means understanding that Christianity gives the truth about the whole of reality, a perspective for interpreting every subject matter."

Nancy Pearcey, Total Truth, Crossway Books, 2004

"The world according to television stands, in nearly every respect, in stark contrast to the way of life put forward in the pages of the Bible."

". . . the most important thing we can communicate to a postmodern world is a coherent and compelling Christian worldview. We have the challenge and privilege of inviting people to occupy with us a biblical way of answering the questions of who made us, why we exist, how we are to live, and what happens when we die."

David W. Henderson, Culture Shift: Communicating God's Truth to our Changing World, Baker Books, 1998

TWO WORLDVIEWS
R. C. SPROUL

As you view the video answer the following:

1. What is a worldview?

2. What is the ultimate division in terms of systems or worldviews?

3. Define:

   a. Theocentric –

   b. Anthropocentric –

4. What is "syncretism"?

5. At what "point" is the conflict between the two systems most clearly seen?

6. What is "nihilism"?

DEVELOPING BIBLICAL ETHICS

CHAPTER 3

Write one ethical question you answered today

Ethics deals with what is right and wrong. Christian ethics deals with what is morally right and wrong for a Christian.

Norman L. Geisler, Christian Ethics, Baker Books, 1989

DEFINITION

eth·ic ($\breve{e}$th ' $\breve{i}$k) *n.*

1. **Philosophy**
   a. A set of principles of right conduct.
   b. A theory or a system of moral values: "An ethic of service is at war with a craving for gain" (Gregg Easterbrook).
2. **ethics** *(used with a sing. verb)* The study of the general nature of morals and of the specific moral choices to be made by a person; moral philosophy.
3. **ethics** *(used with a sing. or pl. verb)* The rules or standards governing the conduct of a person or the members of a profession: *medical ethics*

**The American Heritage® Dictionary of the English Language,
Fourth Edition copyright ©2000 by Houghton Mifflin Company:**

THE BEGINNING OF ETHICS

The Genesis Story: "_____ _____ _____"
(Genesis 1-2)

_____ a Standard

21

What is the Standard?

SCRIPTURE

1 Timothy 4:4-5 For everything God created is good, and nothing is to be rejected if it is received with thanksgiving, because it is consecrated by the word of God and prayer.

Where does the right or good come from?
(Hint: Remember the Biblical Worldview)

THE CHARACTER OF GOD

Essentialism
God wills something because it is good in accord with His nature.
(There is no higher standard of goodness than God's own character and His own approval of what is consistent with His character.)

- God is _____ in His essential nature
Malachi 3:6; James 1:17

- God's essential nature is perfect _____ and _____.
Isaiah 6:3; 1 John 4:8

- God's _____ flows from His _____.
Psalm 145:17; 119:68

His will for our lives is good.
Romans 12:2

THREE BASIC ETHICAL QUESTIONS

excerpts from James M. Grier, Christian Worldview Manual, 1999

1. What _____ I to do?

    Theory of _____

    What am I obligated to do?

    Story:

QUOTATION

...ethics as such is interested less in what people in fact do than in what they ought to do, less in what values presently are and more in what their values ought to be
Arthur F. Holmes Ethics – Approaching Moral Decisions

2. What is _____?

   Theory of _____

   Can Value be defined? Who defines Value? Can Values be checked by a standard?

   Story:

3. Why should I do what is _____?

   Theory of _____

   Can I choose to do good? Why should I choose to do right?

   Story:

A BIBLICAL WORLDVIEW AND ETHICS

A Biblical worldview _____ my ethics.

What I ought to do is _____ _____ _____.

...which means _____.

"I surrender my authority to a higher Authority."

When I surrender my authority and live in obedience,

I _____ what is valuable to me.

and what is valuable _____ me to do what is right and good.

If I do NOT surrender my authority to a higher Authority,

I live in _____, I reveal what is valuable to me,

and what is valuable _____ me to do what is

selfish, wrong and evil or according to the Fall.

As a result of my disobedience to a higher Authority, I must repent

...to live in _____ once again.

If so, I reveal what is valuable to me.

and what is valuable _____ me to live

redemptive or Christianly.

QUOTATION

THE BIBLE ON ETHICS

2 Timothy 3:16-17 (NLT) All Scripture is inspired by God and is useful to teach us what is true and to make us realize what is wrong in our lives. It straightens us out and teaches us to do what is right. It is God's way of preparing us in every way; fully equipped for every good thing God wants us to do.

Romans 2:14-15 (NLT) Even when Gentiles, who do not have God's written law, instinctively follow what the law says, they show that in their hearts they know right from wrong. They demonstrate that God's law is written within them, for their own consciences either accuse them or tell them they are doing what is right.

KNOWING BIBLICAL ETHICS

The process of how we work through moral issues is called an ethical system.

God _____ what is right or good   **Psalm 19:1-6**

In a general way God has revealed, and continues to reveal, His moral will to all humankind   **Romans 1:19-20**

- In _____ this is called

_____ or _____ revelation

We see this evidenced in Man-God's Image has been given moral aptitude.

1. Our _____   **Romans 2:14**

2. Our _____   **Romans 2:15**

DEFINITION

That inward faculty, possessed by all of us which, pronounces judgment upon our attitudes and actions as being either right or wrong, and prompts us to do right.

3. Our _____   **Romans 2:14**

The _____ we have for living.

- In _____   **John 1:1 & 14**

- In _____   **Psalm 19:7-11; John 1:1 & 14**

these are called _____ revelations

1. Its _____.

   - Because of the limits of general revelation.

   - Because humankind needs a final authority for creed and conduct.

INFORMATION

God makes known vital truths about Himself which He has not made known in nature.

2. Its _____.

- It is inspired by God.

- Through it God reveals specialized truth about Himself.

3. Its _____.

- To provide an absolute basis of knowledge concerning the right   **2 Timothy 3:16**

- To change our lives   **2 Timothy 3:17; Ephesians 5:26-27; John 17:17**

4. Its Use

- Abuses of Scripture

    1.

    2.

    3.

    4.

- Its Proper Use

    1. To know _____ _____

        Who He is and who we should be

    2. To know _____ _____   **Psalm 119:1; 1:2**

    3. To give us the _____   **Romans 10:13-17**

    4. To change _____ _____

CHARACTERISTICS OF BIBLICAL ETHICS

- It is based on God's _____ _____.

- It is dependent upon God's _____.

- It is authoritative – It is God "breathed" (inspiration).

- It is prescriptive – It tells us how we should _____.

CHRISTIAN LIBERTY

CHAPTER 4

DEFINITION

lib·er·ty (lĭb'ər-tē) *noun.*

    a.   The condition of being free from restriction or control.
    b.   choosing.
    c.   The condition of being physically and legally free from confinement, servitude, or forced labor.

See synonyms at **freedom**

**The American Heritage® Dictionary of the English Language,
Fourth Edition copyright ©2000 by Houghton Mifflin Company:**

CHRISTIAN LIBERTY: WHAT IT IS?

Christian Liberty is...

...the _____ given by God to assess any issue the Bible does not directly address, without fear of persecution by the church or saints!

QUOTATION

The FREEDOM to make decisions about matters that are not revealed in Scriptures without fear of sinning against God.
Bob DeWaay

QUOTATION

The FREEDOM to function by the internal working of the Spirit. It is being free from having to fulfill the legal code to please God, and free from the frustration of not being able to keep an external set of rules.
Dr. John MacArthur

CHRISTIAN LIBERTY: WHAT IT IS NOT?

Christian Liberty is...

- NOT an excuse to break Biblical Principles.
- NOT an excuse to compromise your conscience.
- NOT an excuse to raise arguments in the church.
- NOT an excuse to do what you want.

SCRIPTURE

1 Corinthians 8:9 But take care that this power of yours does not give cause for trouble to the feeble.

A MODEL OF CHRISTIAN LIBERTY

Christian Liberty in the Garden of Eden

IMAGE was not controlled nor restrained, but voluntarily submitted.

IMAGE was given freedom by God

To make _____ about their lives.

To eat _____ of the things provided.

To _____ names.

IMAGE was given borders to live within that would enhance their freedom. **Genesis 2:8, 15, 17-18**

SCRIPTURE

Genesis 1:27-28 And God made man in his image, in the image of God he made him: male and female he made them. And God gave them his blessing and said to them, Be fertile and have increase, and make the earth full and be masters of it; be rulers over the fish of the sea and over the birds of the air and over every living thing moving on the earth.

SCRIPTURE

Genesis 1:29-30 And God said, "See, I have given you every plant producing seed, on the face of all the earth, and every tree which has fruit producing seed: they will be for your food: And to every beast of the earth and to every bird of the air and every living thing moving on the face of the earth I have given every green plant for food: and it was so.

Genesis 2:16-17 But the LORD told him, "You may eat fruit from any tree in the garden, except the one that has the power to let you know the difference between right and wrong. If you eat any fruit from that tree, you will die before the day is over!"

28

ESSENTIAL DEFINITIONS

Gray Area:

A **gray area** is a term for a border in-between two or more things that is unclearly defined, a border that is hard to define or even impossible to define, or a definition where the distinction border tends to move.

Ethical Gray Area:

A **gray area of ethics** signifies an ethical dilemma, where the border between right and wrong is blurred. Example: *Is killing always abominable?*

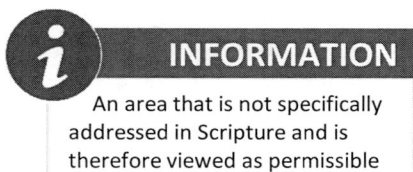

INFORMATION

An area that is not specifically addressed in Scripture and is therefore viewed as permissible

What OUGHT I to do?

		EXAMPLES
Drinking wine	Schooling options	Birth Control
Having a TV	Makeup for Girls	Tattoo/Piercing
Smoking Cigars	Bungee Jumping	Sunday Events
Motorcycles	Coarse Language	Junk Foods

Stronger Brother (or Sister):

One who participates in an ethical gray area in full assurance of his conscience because of his understanding of Christian freedom.

Note: This does not necessarily mean he or she is more mature in the faith than a weaker brother or sister.

Weaker Brother (or Sister):

One who does not participate in an ethical gray area because of the sensitivity of his conscience: his participation would be a sin to him.

Note: This does not necessarily mean he or she is less mature in the faith than a stronger brother or sister.

Stumbling Block:

An action taken by a stronger brother which, though it would ordinarily qualify as a permissible act of freedom, influences a weaker brother to sin against his conscience.

CHRISTIAN LIBERTY APPROACH

1. Principles

   a. _____ about God

      1. If we are confident that what we are engaged in will pass our Lord's scrutiny at the judgment day, we should continue; if not, we should refrain.

      2. Romans 14:6-12

      3. Is He _____ of our lives? He is Lord! Do you accept His lordship in your life?

   b. _____ for ourselves

      1. We must be true to ourselves and not act simply on the opinions of others.

      2. Romans 14:5

      3. Romans 14:22-23

   c. _____ of other believers.

      1. Romans 14:6-21 - Accept one another – vv. 1-3; 15:7.

      2. To "offend" here does not mean to make angry, but rather to cause another believer to act in such a way.

      3. "Am I my brother's keeper?" - Cain! - The spiritual truth is that we are our brother's keeper! (Romans 14:15-20, 15:1-6).

      4. Liberty is great! _____ is better.

      5. We are here to _____ one another, not tear down.

   d. _____

      1. We must maintain and protect it.

      2. John 17

      3. Ephesians 4:3, 11-16

      4. Romans 15:5-13

   e. _____

      1. 1 Corinthians 10:27-33; 11:1

      2. Paul was burdened enough about the unsaved that he restricted himself in doing only what enhanced the gospel in their eyes.

2. Guidelines

   a. **Principle of** _____
      Is this decision GOOD for me? Will it be spiritually profitable? -1 Corinthians 6:12a

   b. **Principle of** _____
      Will this decision CONTROL me? Will it bring me into bondage? -1 Corinthians 6:12b

   c. **Principle of** _____

   d. **Principle of** _____
      Will this decision cause a less MATURE Christian to fall into sin? -1 Corinthians 8:13

   e. **Principle of** _____
      Is this decision BODY or SPIRIT oriented? -1 Corinthians 9:27

   f. **Principle of** _____
      Will this decision give GLORY to God? -1 Corinthians 10:31

 INFORMATION

Perhaps we should see LIBERTY as a gift that is only gained when it is given, not a right as much as a responsibility, and is best exemplified in peace not pride!

BIBLICAL INSIGHTS

Genesis 1-3 - Our Biblical Worldview

Romans 14:1-5 (NIV) - (1) Accept him whose faith is weak, without passing judgment on disputable matters. (2) One man's faith allows him to eat everything, but another man, whose faith is weak, eats only vegetables. (3) The man who eats everything must not look down on him who does not, and the man who does not eat everything must not condemn the man who master he stands or falls. And he will stand, for the Lord is able to make him stand. (5) One man considers one day more sacred than another; another man considers every day alike. Each one should be fully K in his own mind.

1 Corinthians 8:9 (NIV) - Be careful, however, that the exercise of your freedom does not become a stumbling block to the weak.

1 Corinthians 6:12 (NIV) - "Everything is permissible for me"--but not everything is beneficial. "Everything is permissible for me"--but I will not be mastered by anything

CONTEMPORARY
RELIGIOUS WORLDVIEWS
CHAPTER 5

religion [ri-lij-uh n] *noun.*

1. a set of beliefs concerning the cause, nature, and purpose of the universe, especially when considered as the creation of a superhuman agency or agencies, usually involving devotional and ritual observances, and often containing a moral code governing the conduct of human affairs.

2. a specific fundamental set of beliefs and practices generally agreed upon by a number of persons or sects: *the Christian religion; the Buddhist religion.*

3. the body of persons adhering to a particular set of beliefs and practices: *a world council of religions.*

4. the life or state of a monk, nun, etc.: *to enter religion.*

5. the practice of religious beliefs; ritual observance of faith.

6. something one believes in and follows devotedly; a point or matter of ethics or conscience: *to make a religion of fighting prejudice.*

**The American Heritage® Dictionary of the English Language,
Fourth Edition copyright ©2000 by Houghton Mifflin Company:**

A Timeline of the World Religions

1500 B.C.	1000	500	A.D. 0	500	1000	1500	2000

• Hinduism (ca. 1500 B.C.) • Shinto (ca. 660 B.C.) • Christianity (ca. A.D. 30)   • Sikhism (ca. A.D. 1469)

• Judaism (ca. 1440 B.C.) • Zoroastrianism (ca. 630 B.C.)   • Islam (ca. A.D. 622)

• Taoism (ca. 600 B.C.)

• Buddhism (ca. 563 B.C.)

• Confucianism (ca. 551 B.C.)

Halverson, D. (2004) World Religions Overview, International Students, Inc.

WORLD RELIGIONS ORIGIN MAP
http://www.patheos.com/Library/Lenses/Origin-Map.html?&showAll=1

COMPETING RELIGIOUS WORLDVIEWS BIBLICAL CHALLENGE

1 Peter 3:15 (KJV) - But sanctify the Lord God in your hearts: and [be] ready always to [give] an answer to every man that asketh you a reason of the hope that is in you with meekness and fear:

John 14:6 (KJV) - Jesus saith unto him, I am the way, the truth, and the life: no man cometh unto the Father, but by me.

John 17:14-17 (NIV) - I have given them your word and the world has hated them, for they are not of the world any more than I am of the world. [15] My prayer is not that you take them out of the world but that you protect them from the evil one. [16] They are not of the world, even as I a m not of it. [17] Sanctify them by the truth; your word is truth.

THEISM   GOD EXISTS AND IS PERSONALLY AND INTIMATELY INVOLVED WITH HIS CREATION.

ISLAM

[19] Truly, the religion with Allah is Islam. Those who were given the Scripture (Jews and Christians) did not differ except, out of mutual jealousy, after knowledge had come to them. And whoever disbelieves in the Ayat (proofs, evidences, verses, signs, revelations, etc.) of Allah, then surely, Allah is Swift in calling to account. [85] And whoever seeks a religion other than Islam, it will never be accepted of him, and in the Hereafter he will be one of the losers.

Qur'an Surah Aal-'Imran 3:19, 85

1. NAME, KEY SYMBOL AND NUMBER OF FOLLOWERS

A. *Islam, Muslim* -- The word Islam means **"submission"** and refers to the lifestyle of the true "Muslim" (submitter) in submission to the one God's will.

 **QUOTATION**

Islam does not mean "peace" in the Arabic in the classic sense of the term. Islam means "surrender."
Hindson & Caner, Popular Encyclopedia of Apologetics (2008), p. 279

B. The crescent moon and star (see above) – (Origin unknown but generally associated with Islam)

C. Second largest world religion, about 1.5 b. Muslims worldwide (nearly 21% of all religious believers). About 1.6 m. Muslims in the U.S.

2. BRIEF HISTORY

A. An Orphan in Mecca

Muhammad with the Qur'an

1. Raised by paternal uncle - Muhammad (whose name means "highly praised") was born in 570 A.D. in Mecca. His father died before he was born, and his mother when he was six. For two years after that he was raised by his grandfather until he, too, died and his paternal uncle, Abu Talib, raised him in the city of Mecca.
2. Muhammad's marriage – At age 25 he married an older woman named Khadija, a wealthy caravan owner whose caravan he tended.
3. Muhammad's spiritual leanings – Muhammad often retired to a cave interests. He was troubled by the religious practices of the Meccans, especially because of the idolatry and immorality.

B. The Reading/Recitation

1. At age 40 Muhammad, in the month of Ramadan in 610 A.D., while in a cave on Hira, was visited by an angel *Jibril* (Gabriel), holding a scroll. Throughout the rest of his life Muhammad received further revelations. Believing these were, indeed, from God, Muhammad ensured that others wrote down the words he would utter. He often went into trances before uttering the words of the *Qur'an*
2. Allah is One, The chief message At the heart of the *Qur'an's* theology was that God is one, and has no partners or equals, and to believe that he does is the ultimate blasphemy.

C. The Conflict

Although Muhammad's influence was minor at first, more and more people listened and followed his teachings. As his following became larger, more visible and outspoken, the natives of Mecca began to see Muhammad, his teaching and his growing community/brotherhood (*umma*) as a threat and began persecuting them. In the year 622 A.D. Muhammad and his followers left Mecca and went about 280 miles north to *Yathrib* (later called *Medina*; "the city" of the Prophet), and there established Islam as a theocracy. There, the people were far more receptive and eager for Muhammad's message. This exodus from Mecca is called the *Hijrah* or "emigration" and marks the beginning of the Islamic calendar.

D. The Importance of Mecca

Despite his reception and success in Medina, Muhammad still wanted Mecca. The main reason for this was that the Kaaba was in Mecca, the location where, it was believed, Abraham offered Ishmael (not Isaac as the Bible states) to Allah in obedience, symbolizing the ultimate in submission (*islam*) to God.

3. SACRED WRITINGS (THE QUR'AN)

A. *Meaning and Arrangement*

1. "Recitation" – The word *Qur'an* literally means "recitation" and refers to its being revealed to Muhammad and recited by him to be written down and read for all true followers of Allah.
2. 114 surahs (chapters)

B. *Authority*

No "translations"

Islam is not a religion but a way of life

4. CORE THEOLOGY AND PRACTICES OF ISLAM

A. *Five Core Beliefs*

1. The oneness/unity of Allah –
2. The Prophets/Messengers of Islam with primacy on Muhammad -
3. The Scriptures with primacy on the Qur'an –
4. Angelic activity –
5. The Day of Resurrection and Final Judgment –

B. *The Five Pillars of Islam*

1. The Confession of Faith (*Shahada*) -
2. The Contact Prayers (*Salat)*
3. Alms or Poor Tax (*Zakat*) –
4. Fasting during Ramadan –
5. The Pilgrimage to Mecca (*Hajj*) –

The *Shahada* in Arabic

5. DEITY (GOD OR GODS)

Allah
The personal name of God in Aramaic, the language of Jesus and a sister language of Arabic.

Monotheistic
The Prophet Muhammad was asked by his contemporaries about Allah; the answer came directly from God Himself in the form of a short chapter of the Quran, which is considered the essence of the unity or the motto of monotheism.

QUOTATION

The One true God is a reflection of the unique concept that Islam associates with God. To a Muslim, Allah is the Almighty, Creator and Sustainer of the universe, Who is similar to nothing and nothing is comparable to Him. **www.allah.org**

This is chapter 112 which reads:

In the name of God, the Merciful, the Compassionate.
Say (O Muhammad) He is God the One God, the Everlasting Refuge, who has not begotten, nor has been begotten, and equal to Him is not anyone.

Names

Islamic tradition list 99 Names of Allah each of which evoke a distinct characteristic of Allah.
Bentley, D. (1999). The 99 Beautiful Names for God for All the People of the Book.

Characteristic of Allah

Allah of Islam changes.

Surah 2: 106 If We supersede any verse or cause it to be forgotten, We bring a better one or one similar. Do you not know that Allah has power over all things!

Allah is temperamental.

Surah 32: 13:If we so willed, we could have brought every soul its true guidance, but the word from me will come true: 'I will fill Hell with demons and men all together.'

Allah is a deceiver.

Surah 8: 30: They plot and plan, and Allah, too plans, but the best of planners (deceivers) is Allah.

Trinity is blasphemy.

Surah 5: 73: They do blaspheme who say God is one of three…for there is no Allah except one Allah.

Islam believes the Christian trinity is God the Father , God the Mother (Mary) and God the Son (Jesus).

Surah 5: 116: "And behold! God will say: O Jesus the son of Mary didst say unto men, 'worship me and my mother as gods' in derogation of Allah?

6. SUMMARIZING ISLAM'S PLAN OF SALVATION

A. *What is salvation?* – Entering Paradise on Judgment Day, and escaping Hell

B. *What makes salvation necessary?* – Humanity's forgetfulness/ignorance of Allah's Oneness and the Qur'an; and sure damnation if Allah is not remembered and obeyed.

C. *What makes salvation possible?* – Revelation of the *Qur'an* to Muhammad; it is called, among other things a "mercy" and a "guide' to humanity to find submission, the true religion.

D. *What makes salvation personal?* – Submission to Allah as demonstrated by strict adherence to the Five Pillars.

7. ISLAM SINCE MUHAMMAD

A. *Death of Muhammad and Division of Muslims*

1. *The Sunnis*
2. *The Shiites*

   The two major sects of Islam, Sunni and Shi'ite, were divided originally over a dispute as to who should serve as the first *caliph*, or successor, to Muhammad, who had failed to appoint one before his death. The Sunni Muslims insisted that Muhammad's successor should be elected. The Shi'ite (or Shia'h) Muslims thought he should come through Muhammad's bloodline, which would have meant Ali, Muhammad's cousin and son-in-law, would be his successor.

B. *Islam and Jihad*

8. SOME BIBLICAL PERSPECTIVE ON ISLAM

Of the three faiths we have examined, Islam is closest to Christianity. In fact, as we have mentioned, the *Qur'an* even speaks very highly of Jesus, but while this is the case, it does not honor Jesus as God, which the Bible says, clearly, we are to do (John 5:23).   Let's briefly examine this Jesus question, and demonstrate how Islam and Christianity are not teaching the same thing at all when it comes to the true worship of God and why this even matters.

In the *Qur'an, surah* 3:42-60 we find a very lengthy teaching about Jesus, much of which is consistent with the Gospels. His birth was preannounced to Mary, he was born of a virgin, He will be obeyed and teach obedience to the disciples (meaning they were Muslims, of course), he performed miracles like healing lepers, the blind and raising the dead! (a claim Muhammad could not make). Jesus was "faultless!" (v.19:19, another thing true about Jesus, but not Muhammad), and "a revelation" and a "mercy" and that all this was "ordained." (v.21) Jesus unlike any other messenger of Allah, was said to be "supported/strengthened . . . with the holy Spirit." (2:253, 5:110). Jesus alone, was given "the Gospel" (5:46, 57:27) . Jesus is regularly identified in the *Qur'an* as "Messiah" which no other prophet, including Muhammad, is designated.

Despite these amazingly positive, and even biblical things said about Jesus, the *Qur'an* denies two very central biblical teachings which happens to undermine the essence of Christianity. According to *surah* 4:157-158 Jesus was not crucified, but in a sleight of hand, Allah made it "appear" that the Jews had slain Jesus. Instead, Allah "took him up" to himself (although we don't know exactly what this means). Messiah's/Christ's literal death is central to the Bible (Isaiah 53 and 1 Corinthians) and the heart of the gospel. Christianity is nothing without the crucifixion of Christ, and His unique resurrection "from the dead."

More troubling, however, is the *Qur'an's* blatant denial of Jesus' deity. Of course this grows out of the doctrine of Allah's oneness, making it impossible that he could have equal "partners" in heaven. A related idea attacked by this is Jesus' being the "son" of God. According to the *Qur'an*, God cannot have a son (2:116, 4:171, 6:101) and that there is "no warrant" (10:68), for such a claim. To suggest this is "a disastrous thing" with potentially devastating cosmic effects (19:88-93). In fact, at some points Jesus, the Messiah, son of Mary (as the *Qur'an* frequently refers to him), is the very one who denies his own Sonship and deity, pronouncing severe judgment on any who would suggest otherwise (5:72-3). It follows from this that Jesus was "no other than a messenger," indistinct from all previous messengers (2:136, 4:171), and nothing other than a human, just like Adam (3:59), which, of course, annuls any idea of Jesus' pre-existence. Jesus accepted his status as a mere "slave" of Allah (19:30, 33, 43:59; like we all should), and even predicts the coming of Muhammad, whose name would be "even more praised" (61:6) than his.

To answer this challenge we need to compare/contrast the biblical view of Jesus, and what He claimed about himself, to the Qur'an's depiction of Jesus. For sake of time, we will limit this analysis to the Gospel of John in which Jesus' deity is unequivocally proclaimed with a purpose to guide us into believing that He is the Christ, the son of God, and that believing we might have life in His name (John 20:31).

(1:1-2,). The Word was the agent of creation of all things, including the world (1:3, 10 see also Colossians 1:16-17 and Hebrews 1:2). The eternal Word which dwelt with God and was God and which created all things was "made flesh and dwelt among us" and was the "son" who made the Father known to the world during his earthly sojourn (1:18, see also Colossians 1:19, 2:9 and Hebrews 1:3). This remarkable passage has already established Jesus' pre-existence, His equality with God, His being the creator of all things, and His Sonship, making known "the Father" to the world; all things denied by the Qur'an. The rest of John's gospel clearly establishes Jesus' Sonship and deity, and that this is the critical issue for humans to believe so that they might, be forgiven of their sins, and have eternal life.

The self-understanding of Jesus we find in the Bible is clearly poles apart from that which we see in the *Qur'an*. As we have seen, in the gospel of John alone Jesus explicitly claims to be the "Son of God" (which is equivalent to a claim to deity), and to have pre-existed with the "Father" "in heaven" prior to His appearance on earth. He claims to have "come from heaven" and not to have originated in the world like all humans, He asserts his sinlessness, and how this qualifies His doctrine as authoritative and certifies his oneness with God. He also predicts his literal death and its purpose, and explains that he, as God alone, has the power to forgive sins. Jesus Christ and His message about Himself as the Son of God and the one in whom we must place our saving faith is all that matters.

Islam and Christianity Contrasted

Islam	Christianity
God	
A singular unity. No partner is to be associated with God.	A compound unity; one in essence, three in person.
Humanity	
Good by nature.	Sinful by nature.
Sin	
Sin is thought of in terms of rejecting right guidance. It can be forgiven through repentance. No atonement is necessary.	Sin is serious (Rom. 6:23, Eph. 2:1). It reflects an attitude of moral rebellion against the holy God, which causes us to be alienated from Him. An atonement is necessary.
Salvation	
The standard for salvation is having one's good deeds outweigh the bad. Therefore, it is based on human effort.	The standard for salvation is the absolute holiness of God (Matt. 5:48). Therefore, it can only be offered as a gift through the grace of God and received through faith.
Jesus	
One of the major prophets. To associate Jesus with God (i.e., to call Him the Son of God) is blasphemy. Muslims affirm the virgin birth of Jesus and the miracles that He performed.	The one and only Son of God. John wrote, "Who is the liar? It is the man who denies that Jesus is the Christ. Such a man is the antichrist—he denies the Father and the Son" (1 John 2:22).
The Death of Christ	
According to Islamic tradition, Jesus did not die on the cross. Instead, He went to heaven, and Judas died in His place on the cross. Muslims believe that it is disrespectful to believe that God would allow one of his prophets—and especially one of the most honored of the prophets—to be crucified.	Jesus died a physical death as a substitute for our sins. He then rose from the dead in a physical but immortal body and appeared to hundreds of witnesses (1 Cor. 15). God's specific purpose for sending Jesus into the world was for Him to be crucified and to die for our sins (Matt. 20:28; John 3:16; Rom. 8:3; 2 Cor. 5:21; 1 Pet. 1:19-20). Jesus voluntarily gave His life for us (John 6:51; 10:11-17). The end was not that of dishonor but that of the highest exaltation (Acts 2:29-33; 5:30-31; Phil. 2:8-11).
The Bible	
Corrupted. Abrogated by the Qur'an.	Authentic. Divinely inspired. The final authority in all matters of faith and truth.

PANTHEISM GOD AND THE UNIVERSE ARE THE SAME THING.

HINDUISM

> "Abandon all varieties of religion and just surrender unto Me. I shall deliver you from all sinful reactions. Do not fear."
> Lord Krishna, Bhagavad-Gita 18:66

1. NAME, KEY SYMBOL AND NUMBER OF FOLLOWERS

A. Dharma – righteousness, duty; "Hinduism" a later word applied to people of Indus Valley, now accepted by natives.

B. Meaning of symbol "*OM*"

C. The **third largest world religion**; roughly 900 million Hindus worldwide (14% of all religious adherents) and about 1 million in U. S.

2. BRIEF HISTORY

A. The Vedic Period (1500 to 300 B.C. – no one really knows)

B. The Upanishads (800-400 B.C.)

C. Modern Hinduism - Unlike Buddhism, Christianity and Islam, Hinduism has no single founder, and it is also impossible to say exactly what Hinduism is in terms of religious beliefs because there is no one way of understanding "god."

3. SACRED WRITINGS

A. The Vedas

1. Largely polytheistic; worship of many gods (symbolizing natural forces).
2. Brahmanism (leadership by priests) predominant – custodians of elaborate and tedious sacrificial system to thank and appease gods. (*Brahmanas* – priestly manuals)
3. Philosophy of *Upanishads*, also called *Vedanta* ("end" of the Vedas) more prominent in Hinduism today. Only Hindu scholars learn and study *Vedas* now.

B. The Upanishads

1. Philosophical basis of Hinduism today.
2. Essentially philosophical commentaries on the rest of the Vedic writings.
3. Teach *advaita, or* "non-dualist" view of the universe (no spirit and matter, just all spirit (*Brahman*)

4. More characteristically monistic (non-dualistic/pantheistic), conveying the idea that all
    (a) Reality is in essence *One—Brahman*, which manifests itself in the many
    (b) powers or gods, and is the true essence of all things. Polytheism.
5. Central idea - *"Atman is Brahman"* summed up in **"tat tvam asi,"** *lit. "You are That."*

C. The Epics

1. Mahabharata *(Between 540 and 300 B.C. "The great Bharata" – a family name)*
2. Bhagavad-*Gita (Bet. 1000-900 B.C.; Lit. "Song of the Supreme Lord;" Abbreviate "Gita"*) - 18 chapters of Book 6 of *Mahabharata* Featuring Lord Krishna (eighth *avatar* of Vishnu), a very popular deity in modern Hinduism.
3. Main subjects of the *Gita,*
    (a) Way of salvation explained from philosophy of Upanishads.
    (b) Indestructibility of the Atman and its oneness with Brahman
    (c) Duties (dharma) of caste
    (d) Karma, samsara and moksha,
    (e) Supreme value of yoga (especially karma and bhakti)
    (f) Krishna reveals self as Supreme Being over all gods and people (Gita 4.06, 10).

4. CORE BELIEFS OF HINDU SCRIPTURES

Important: This is not a creed or "doctrinal statement" for determining whether someone is or is not a Hindu. They are not required beliefs, but presently beliefs held by most Hindus.

A. Brahman – Most Hindus believe that ultimate Reality is *Brahman*

B. Atman
All humans possess an *atman*, or eternal and indestructible soul/self and its ultimate destiny and purpose is to be united to *Brahman* the true Self.
Note: Realizing that *atman is Brahman* is to achieve the highest or perfect knowledge, according to Hinduism.

C. Maya
Our perceptions are actually *maya*, which means "illusion" or "appearance;" that is, what we experience in our existence, in the natural worlds, is not the really real, kind of like a dream or a mirage—it appears real and we may act as though it is real, but it is an illusion, it is an "illusive power" (*Gita* 3.29)

D. Samsara

We are caught up in the illusory world of *maya* because of our desires and attachments to the world and its pleasures. As long as the *atman* does not realize that it is really *Brahman*, it remains locked in the potentially endless earthly cycle of birth, death and rebirth called *samsara*, or literally "a wandering across."

Samsara: **The endless cycles of death and rebirth**

E. Karma – The law of *karma* (cause and effect based on actions/deeds)

- Keeps people locked in *samsara* (even "good" karma).
- Depending on *karma*, may be reincarnated (or return in another physical body) as a human, an animal or even a plant.
- Good karma still a curse, but has some benefits
- Temporary heavenly time, then reincarnation in higher caste (thus one step closer to *moksha*)

F. Moksha/Nirvana – The hope in Hinduism, the salvation for which Hindus strive, is *moksha*. This is "liberation" from *samsara*.

G. Caste - This was a hierarchy of social privilege and responsibility based on one's *karma* from a past life. (*Gita* 18.41-44).

- to their caste.
- Karma determines *caste* and *caste* determines *dharma*.
- Divinely established system (*Gita* 18.41-44 also *Laws of Manu*—the first man; have detailed explanations of caste). Four original castes, with a fifth added. Hundreds of *sub castes* in India today. Castes are not to socialize or intermarry.
  - *Brahmin* – religious leaders/teachers and nobility
  - *Kshatriya* – military and administrators of society
  - *Vaishyas* – manual laborers, like craftsmen, farmers and merchants
  - *Shudras* - duty (*dharma*) it was to serve the higher castes
  - *Dalit* – In time, Hindus also identified another caste, the *dalit* or "untouchables," who were the lowest of the low in terms of poverty and lack of privilege.

5. DIETY (GOD OR GODS)

Brahman

While Hindus believe in *Brahman* and define this as the Supreme and Absolute Reality; the Eternal, the Infinite and the Indivisible Existence, the Self, they also believe that *Brahman* manifests itself in "various powers" these being the many gods and goddesses of Hinduism. Hindus may, therefore, claim that there is only one god, *Brahman*, or any number of the hundreds of millions of lesser deities that they devote themselves to in hopes to achieve *moksha*. This is

In modern Hinduism there are three main deities the *Trimurti or "triad"* (but essentially 300 m. deities and sub deities as well!).

- o Brahma (the Creator),
- o Vishnu (the Preserver),
- o Siva (the Destroyer)

brahma   vishnu   shiva

6. SUMMARIZING HINDUISM'S PLAN OF SALVATION:

A. ***What is salvation?*** – *Moksha* – liberation from *samsara* Main idea—performing daily duties (dharma) and disciplines in view of union (yoking) with *Brahman.*

B. ***What makes salvation necessary?*** – *Karma* and *samsara* – We are locked into this never-ending cycle because we have not renounced earthly pleasures and sought union with Brahman. We are ignorant of this true knowledge which keeps us trapped in the illusion.

C. especially the *Gita* where Krishna tells his followers how to be united to Brahman; the Supreme.

D. ***What makes salvation personal?*** – Renunciation of earthly pleasures, fulfilling *dharma (caste duty)*, practicing *yoga* (focusing mind and body on achieving union with Brahman)

7. SOME BIBLICAL PERSPECTIVE ON HINDUISM

Some claim that Hinduism is the "oldest" of the world religions, suggesting it's the beginning of man's religious thought. Christians would have to disagree with this. In Genesis we see the oldest human "religion" and civilization. Biblical narrative conveys that there is one God who created humans in His image and likeness as one male and one female initially; these first humans then fell into corruption. They acquired a sin nature which somehow affected their heart which became "evil only continually." But God promised redemption to these humans and covered their original sins with animal skins, instituting the need for sacrificial atonement to pay for sin. When humanity became utterly corrupt, God destroyed the world through a worldwide, catastrophic flood, after which Noah's family became the basis of all current civilizations, including that which settled in the Indus Valley. In Genesis Chapter 10 we see how from Noah and his sons descended all the nations (10:32). In chapter 11 we learn how the world was populated from the incident at Babel. Languages changed and people dispersed.

Once these early ancestors spread out, they took ideas of the true religion—the true story of many other parts of the world, they eventually, due to their sin nature, distorted these ideas into polytheism - assigning separate gods to the parts of creation (which early Hinduism did)—but still retained ideas consistent with a biblical theology; like an *original creation*, a *worldwide flood, moral obligations*, etc. Paul, in fact, states clearly that *humanity has always known the truth about God, but, due to their sinfulness, suppressed that truth*, and "exchanged the truth of God for a lie, and worshipped and served the creature more than the Creator (Romans 1:19-25)." The multiple depictions of Hindus gods as animals, humans and mixtures of both, is part of the distortion when they "changed the glory of the incorruptible God into images of corruptible man, and birds and four-footed beasts and creeping things (Romans 1:23).

We should not be surprised that we find similarities in religions like Hinduism, because God created the human heart (Psalm 33:15) and placed eternity (Ecclesiastes 3:11) and a sense of morality (Romans 2:14-15) in it. Religions, thus, always convey morality (and very similar ones at that) and a sense of eternal life no matter where they are in the world; what we might call a sense of always (a yearning for immortality) and a sense of ought (an inescapable sense of moral law).

Hinduism and Christianity Contrasted

Hinduism	Christianity
God	
Impersonal.	Personal.
Humanity	
Continuous in the sense of being extended from the being of God.	Discontinuous in the sense of being separate from the Being of God; continuous in the sense of being made in God's image.
Humanity's Problem	
Ignorance	Moral rebellion.
The Solution	
Liberation from illusion and ignorance.	Forgiveness of sin and reconciliation with the personal holy God.
The Means	
Detachment from desire and awareness of unity with the divine through self effort.	Repentance from sin and trusting in the completed and substitutionary work of Jesus Christ.
The Outcome	
Merge into the Oneness; the individual disappears.	Eternal fellowship with God; the person is fulfilled in a loving relationship with God.

PANTHEISM GOD AND THE UNIVERSE ARE THE SAME THING.

BUDDHISM

1. NAME , KEY SYMBOL AND NUMBER OF FOLLOWERS

> The best of all paths is the Eightfold Path. The best of all truths are the Four Noble Truths. Non-attachment is the best of all states. The best of all men is the Seeing One (the Buddha). This is the only Way. There is none other for the purity of vision. Everything else is . . . deceit"
>
> The Buddha, Dhamappada 20:273-274

A. *Buddha* and *Buddhism*

B. The Wheel of Dharma (or Dhamma), or Dharma/Dhamma Wheel

C. Fourth largest world religion, 488 million Buddhists worldwide, representing 7% of the world's total population

QUOTATION

The sole purpose of Buddhist teachings is to develop our mind and hearts in terms of inner growth. Buddhism is nothing but a way or method to work on our inner or spiritual development. Through its teachings we try to change and transform the way we are, as well as the way we see ourselves and everything around us.

Tulku, Daring Steps: Traversing the path of Buddha (2010), p. 13

2. BRIEF HISTORY

A. A Renegade Hindu
   - A royal birthright Buddhism was founded by Siddhartha Gautama during the sixth century B.C. His life (563-483 B.C.) coincides with the time when the people of Judah were exiled in Babylon.
   - Four Signs
   - The Great Renunciation

B. Discovering the Middle Path
   - Life offers only *dukkha,* -
   - Six years of asceticism -
   - The Middle Path/*Dhamma* -

SOURCE

BUDDHISM INFORMATION

- The wheel is one of the most important Buddhist symbols, as it represents the teachings of the Buddha. The Buddha was the one who "turned the wheel of the dharma" and thus the wheel symbol is the Dharmachakra, or "wheel of law"

- The wheel's motion is a metaphor for the rapid spiritual change engendered by the teachings of the Buddha.

- The wheel also represents the endless cycle of samsara, or rebirth, which can only be escaped by means of the Buddha's teachings.

http://www.religionfacts.com/buddhism

3. CENTRAL PRINCIPLES AND PRACTICES OF BUDDHISM

THE FOUR NOBLE TRUTHS

A. The First Noble Truth (The certainty of suffering):

Life consists of suffering (dukkha). This concept of suffering includes the experiences of pain, misery, sorrow, and unfulfillment.

B. The Second Noble Truth (The source/cause of suffering):

Everything is impermanent and ever-changing (the doctrine of *anicca*). We suffer because we desire those things that are impermanent.

C. The Third Noble Truth (The cessation/cure of suffering):

The way to liberate oneself from suffering is by eliminating all desire. We must stop craving that which is temporary.

D. The Fourth Noble Truth (The path to the cessation of suffering):

Desire can be eliminated by following the Eightfold Path, which consists of eight points that can be categorized according to three major sections:

THE PRACTICE OF BUDDHISM (The Noble Eightfold Path)

Wisdom (*Panna*)

1. **Right Understanding**
2. **Right Thought**

Ethical Conduct (*Sila*)

3. **Right Speech**
4. **Right Action**
5. **Right Livelihood**

Mental Discipline (*Smadhi*)

6. **Right Effort**
7. **Right Awareness**
8. **Right Meditation**

> These eight points are not steps to be taken in sequential order, but are attitudes and actions to be developed simultaneously
> The first two points, moreover, serve as the foundation from which the other points flow.

FURTHER PRINCIPLES OF BUDDHISM

Nirvana *in Buddhism (The Goal)*

- Not heaven or paradise, not a place that one goes when they die
- A passionless state where one feels neither love nor hate
- Literal meaning of Nirvana

4. SACRED WRITINGS

Tripitaka - The "Three Baskets"

    A. *Sutta-Pitaka* -
- The *Dhamapadda**
- The *Jatakas* -

    B. *Abhidhamma Pitaka*

5. BECOMING A BUDDHIST

It has become quite common in Buddhism to speak of the Three Jewels or Refuges of:

A. The *Buddha* – What he experienced and the example he left behind

B. The *Dhamma* - What the Buddha taught; The "Way of Truth"

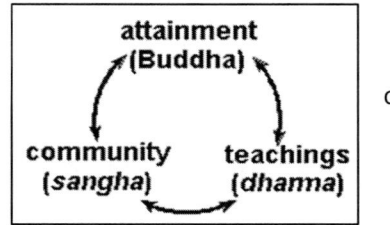

C. The *Sangha* – The community of followers Buddha established who have chosen to follow the Buddha's **Note:** Becoming a Buddhist does not require any official ceremony; but often when a would-be follower recited the phrase; "I go for refuge in the Buddha, I go for refuge in the Dhamma and I go for refuge in the Sangha." They would be considered having started on the path of a Buddhist, on their way to freedom from suffering.

6. SUMMARIZING BUDDHISM'S PLAN OF SALVATION

A. *What is salvation?* – Liberation from suffering and what causes it, achieving Nirvana

B. *What makes salvation necessary?* – Potentially endless cycles of rebirth and death (samsara)

C. teachings

D. *What makes salvation personal?* – Believing the Four Noble Truths and practicing the Noble Eightfold Path.

7. SOME BIBLICAL PERSPECTIVE ON BUDDHISM

Some suggest that Jesus and Buddha really taught essentially the same things, that their doctrines are compatible. This is both true in not true in this way. From an ethical perspective, Buddhism has a lot of merit in that Gautama's and Jesus' moral doctrines are similar. This, we could attribute to the moral law of God "written on the heart" (Romans 2:14-15) and should not find it surprising that all religions, not just Buddhism, teach very similar moral principles. Because of this, much of the ethical teaching and stories of Gautama can be illuminating and illustrative to Jesus' followers.

But here is where the comparison ends. Theologically, Jesus and Gautama are at two opposite poles. Jesus was a monotheist and believed in and taught that God was personal and could be related to as intimately as a "Father" who created man and woman in his image and sustains His creation in a very active way. Jesus taught and modeled prayer to the Father. His use of the intimate term "Abba" is quite significant in this regard. (Mk 14:36) He teaches his followers to pray "Our Father Who is in Heaven (Matthew 6:9) this intimacy with God as a personal, heavenly Father is also taught by Paul (Romans 8:15, Galatians 4:6).

Jesus also believed the source of our sorrows came from within, due to an indwelling sin nature and core corruption, not merely desire or craving (Mark 7:21-22). So a huge and significant contrast is that Jesus taught that we needed to be forgiven of sin by our Heavenly Father (Matthew 6:12). He also taught about the Kingdom of Heaven as though it were a place in the afterlife that one could aspire to and dwell in, as well as a present reality (Matthew 5:20), and thus escape the condemnation of a literal hell, about which He taught and warned even more than He did heaven. Jesus also spoke of death and resurrection and a final judgment (John 5:29), never reincarnation.

Probably of the greatest significance is the contrast in how Jesus and Gautama thought of themselves and their importance for humanity. Gautama told his followers not to remember him, *per se,* but his teachings as the most important thing. In fact, contrary to popular opinion, Gautama was quite adamant that his teachings were superior to all others. He taught, "The best of ways is the eightfold; the best of truths the four words (noble truths); the best of virtues passionlessness. *This is the way, there is no other* that leads to the purifying of intelligence. Go on this way! Everything else is . . . deceit. (*Dhamapadda* 20:273-4). Jesus, on the other hand did not point to his teachings as "the way" but rather to Himself as *the* way, *the* truth and *the* life." (John 14:6) His disciples/apostles followed suit when they pronounced "neither is there salvation in any other, for there is no other name under heaven given among men by which we must be saved" (Acts 4:12)

This cannot be overemphasized. While Jesus was humble and considered one wise who built his life on His teachings (Matthew 7:24-27), He unequivocally conveyed that getting his identity right was critical to our eternal well-being. "Who do you say that I am?" (Matthew 16:15), "If you do not believe that I am He, you will die in your sins." (John 8:24) "He who does not believe the Son does not have life . . . but God's wrath abides on him." (John 3:18) and "No one comes to the Father except through me." (John 14:6). Jesus made it clear that remembering Him (Luke 22:19) and believing in Him alone for salvation was critical to being His follower and entering the kingdom of Heaven to live eternally with God; there was no other way. So while Gautama taught high moral principles, and claimed to point the way, leaving us some great quotes and illustrations, Jesus Christ was far more than a great moral teacher, and claimed to *be* the way.

Buddhism and Christianity Contrasted

	Theravada Buddhism	Mahayana Buddhism	Christianity
God	*Nirvana*, an abstract Void.	*Nirvana*, an abstract Void, but also an undifferentiated Buddha essence.	A personal God who is self-existent and changeless.
Humanity	An impermanent collection of aggregates.	An impermanent collection of aggregates. For some, personal existence continues for awhile in the Pure Land.	Made in God's image. Personal existence has value. We continue to exist as persons after death.
The Problem	We suffer because we desire that which is temporary, and we continue in the illusion of the existence of the self.	Same as Theravada.	We suffer because of the consequences of our sin. But we also suffer because, being made in God's image, we are fulfilled only when we are in a relationship with our Creator God. But we have rebelled against God, and are thus alienated from Him.
The Solution	To cease all desire and to realize the nonexistence of the self, thus finding permanence.	To become aware of the Buddha-nature within.	To be forgiven by and reconciled with God. We find permanence in the immutability of God.
The Means	Self-reliance. We must follow the Middle Path, and accrue karmic merit.	Self-reliance. The means vary from following the Eightfold Path, to emptying the mind, to accruing merit by performing rituals, to realizing the Buddha-nature within, to depending on the merits of a *bodhisattva*.	Reliance on God. We must repent of our sins and trust in the saving work of Jesus Christ.
The Outcome	To enter *nirvana* where the ego is extinguished.	The outcome varies from that of returning as a *bodhisattva* in order to guide others, to living in a Pure Land from which one can enter *nirvana*, to entering *nirvana*.	Our existence as individuals survives death, and we are fulfilled as we are in eternal fellowship with a loving and personal God.

SALVATION COMPARISON CHART

	Islam ☪	Buddhism ☸	Hinduism ॐ	Christianity
WHAT IS SALVATION?	Being **rewarded** on Judgment Day with entrance into Paradise if one's righteous deeds are determined to outweigh their sinful deeds	Achievement of *Nirvana* – "**Cessation**" of desire and the suffering that comes from desire, including the cycles of death and rebirth.	Achievement of *Moksha* - "**Liberation**" from the painful cycle of death and rebirth. **Realization** of one's unity with Ultimate Reality (*Brahman*)	Being **rescued** from sin's eternal consequences, temporal control and actual condition. **Receiving** eternal life as **a gift of grace**
WHAT MAKES SALVATION NECESSARY?	Humans are ignorant of their true nature as a Muslim (submitter) and destined for Hell's fire until they submit to Allah's will	Humans are **enslaved** by *karma* to *samsara* **because of** their **desire** for the impermanent things of this world, and experience endless **suffering** due to this.	Humans, because of *karma*, are trapped in the cycle of death and rebirth (*samsara*) because of their **ignorance** of Ultimate Reality, and attachment to worldly illusion (*maya*)	Humans are **sinful**, and are **separated** from and **subject to the eternal wrath** of a Holy and Righteous God
WHAT MAKES SALVATION POSSIBLE?	The *Qur'an* which teaches humans of their true identity as Muslims who must willingly submit to the will of Allah..	The enlightenment, **example and teachings of Siddhartha Gautama** who became the Buddha through overcoming his desire.	The **knowledge** found in the Hindu Scriptures about escaping *karma* and *samsara* and achieving *moksha* and one's ultimate unity with *Brahman.*	*Divine initiative:* God through **love** and **grace** reveals the **gospel** and provides to rescue humans from sin through the substitutionary **death and resurrection of Jesus Christ.**
WHAT MAKES SALVATION PERSONAL?	*Human Effort:* **Confessing** the *Shahada;* believing the **Articles of Faith** and practicing the **Five Pillars of Islam.**	*Human Effort:* Accepting the **Four Noble Truths** and following the **Noble Eightfold Path.** Taking refuge in the Buddha, *Dhamma* (his teachings) and *Sangha* (community of fellow Buddhists).	*Human effort:* **Becoming a yogi** (one who practices yoga, a discipline by which can realize oneness with Ultimate Reality); **Living faithfully** to one's given station in life (*caste* and *dharma*).	**Repentance and faith;** Owning up to and turning from one's sin and turning to the Savior, Jesus Christ, alone for salvation and submitting to him as the Lord.
WHAT IS THE RELATIONSHIP BETWEEN SALVATION AND MORALITY?	**Salvation** (earning Paradise) possible only **through** faithfully living **a moral life** as defined by *Qur'an* and *Sunnah to be* determined on Judgment Day.	**Salvation is the result of** rigorously living **a moral life** as articulated in the Noble Eightfold Path and the Five precepts (Ten precepts if a monk or nun).	**Salvation** (*moksha*) is **the result of a moral life**, but especially being a yogi and following the discipline of yoga to focus in union with Brahman.	The **moral life is the result of salvation.** When one receives Christ they are empowered through the Holy spirit to live as they ought and to please God by following Jesus' moral example.

UNDERSTANDING TOLERANCE

CHAPTER 6

DEFINITION

tol·er·ance (tŏl′ər-əns) *noun.*

1. The capacity for or the practice of recognizing and respecting the beliefs or
   a. Leeway for variation from a standard.
   b. The permissible deviation from a specified value of a structural dimension, often expressed as a percent.
2. The capacity to endure hardship or pain.

Dictionary.com from The American Heritage® Dictionary of the English Language, Fourth Edition copyright ©2000 by Houghton Mifflin Company:

to recognize and respect [other's beliefs, practices, etc.] without sharing them and to bear or put up with [someone or something not especially liked].

Webster's® New Collegiate Dictionary, Fourth Edition copyright ©1980 by G. & C. Merriman Company:

Note: To tolerate implies that we disagree. We don't "tolerate" people or ideas that share our views because there is nothing to "put up with".

THOUGHTS ON TOLERANCE

"Contrary to popular definitions, true tolerance means 'putting up with error' – not 'being accepting of all views.' We don't tolerate what we enjoy or approve of . . . by definition what we tolerate is what we disapprove of or we believe to be false and erroneous . . . if disagreement didn't exist, then tolerance would be unnecessary."

Paul Copan, True for You but not for Me, 1998, p. 35

"Dialogue thus becomes an opportunity for both sides to reexamine their presuppositions and clarify their positions. True tolerance grants people the right to dissent."

Paul Copan, True for You but not for Me, 1998, p. 36

"Civility," is at the heart of the classical view of tolerance. It can be loosely equated with the word "respect." Tolerance applies to how we treat people we disagree with, not how we treat ideas we think are false. We respect those who hold different beliefs from our own by treating such people courteously and allowing their views a place in the public discourse. We may strongly disagree with their ideas and vigorously contend against them in the public square, but we still show respect to their persons despite our differences.

Gregory Koukl, The Intolerance of Tolerance

TYPES OF TOLERANCE

1. Traditional Tolerance

Tolerance is a word that applies to how we treat _____ we disagree with, _____ how we treat _____ we think false.

a. _____ and protecting the legitimate rights of others, even those with whom you disagree and those who are different from you.

b. Listening to and learning from other perspectives, cultures, and backgrounds.

c. Living _____ alongside others, in spite of differences.

d. _____ other people, regardless of their race, creed, nationality, or sex.

e. Traditional tolerance _____, _____, and _____ the individual without the necessarily approving of or participating in his/her or beliefs or behaviors.

2. The New Tolerance

To be truly tolerant, you must agree that _____ _____ _____ _____ as your own. You must give your approval, your endorsement, your sincere support to their _____ and _____.

a. The new tolerance may sound like traditional tolerance, but it is vastly different.

It is based on the belief that "truth is _____ to the community in which a person participates. And since there are many human communities, there are necessarily many _____ truths."

"Since truth is described by language, and all language is created by humans, all truth is created by humans."
If all truth is created by humans, and all humans are "created equal," then all truth is _____.

b. In contrast to traditional tolerance, which asserts that everyone has an equal right to _____ or say what he thinks is right, the new tolerance says that what every individual believes or says is _____ right, _____ valid.

3. Zero Tolerance

A non-flexible enforcement policy for the criminal law or _____ _____. Under a system of zero tolerance, persons in positions of authority--who might other-wise exercise their discretion in making _____ judgments regarding the severity of a given offense–are instead _____ to act in particular ways and, where relevant, to impose a _____ _____ regardless of individual culpability.

BIBLICAL INSIGHTS

The Bible makes it clear that all values, beliefs, lifestyles, and truth claims are not equally valid.

1. It teaches that the God of the Bible is the _____ God.
   Jeremiah 10:10

2. All of His words are _____ .
   Psalm 119:160; Deuteronomy 6:18

QUOTATION

"Notice that one can't tolerate someone unless he disagrees with him. We don't "tolerate" people who share our views. They're on our side. There's nothing to put up with. Tolerance is reserved for those we think are wrong.

This essential element of tolerance--disagreement--has been completely lost in the modern distortion of the concept. Nowadays, if you think someone is wrong, you're called intolerant.

This presents us with a very curious problem. Judging someone wrong makes one intolerant, yet one must first think another is wrong in order to be tolerant. It's a "Catch-22." According to this approach, true tolerance is impossible.

Greg Koukl, www.str.org

THE COST OF TOLERANCE

Proponents of the new tolerance have no problem being _____ to Christians, Christianity, and Christian morality because those things present problems for the new tolerance in four basic areas:

1. _____

2. _____ and the Cross

3. _____

4. The _____ of the Church

got tolerance?

TOLERANCE AND THE CHRISTIAN

The Bible makes it clear how Christians are to act toward each other and toward those outside of the faith:

a. Romans 12:16   Principle: _____

b. Romans 12:18   Principle: _____

c. Ephesians 4:2   Principle: _____

d. Ephesians 4:32   Principle: _____

e. Colossians 3:13   Principle: _____

f. Galatians 6:10   Principle: _____

In all this we must still stand up for and speak the TRUTH in love

BIBLICAL INFORMATION

1 Peter 3:15-16 (NLT) Instead, you must worship Christ as Lord of your life. And if you are asked about your Christian hope, always be ready to explain it. (16) But you must do this in a gentle and respectful way. Keep your conscience clear. Then if people speak evil against you, they will be ashamed when they see what a good life you live because you belong to Christ.

Ephesians 4:14-15 (NLT) Then we will no longer be like children, forever changing our minds about what we believe because someone has told us something different or because someone has cleverly lied to us and made the lie sound like the truth. [15]Instead, we will hold to the truth in love, becoming more and more in every way like Christ, who is the head
Romans 12:18 (NIV) If it is possible, as far as it depends on you, live at peace with everyone.

Romans 1:15-16 (NIV) That is why I am so eager to preach the gospel also to you who are at Rome. I am not ashamed of the gospel, because it is the power of God for the salvation of everyone who believes: first for the Jew, then for the Gentile.

2 Timothy 2:24-26 (NLT) The Lord's servants must not quarrel but must be kind to everyone. They must be able to teach effectively and be patient with difficult people. They should gently teach those who oppose the truth. Perhaps God will change those people's hearts, and they will believe the truth. [26]Then they will come to their senses and escape from the Devil's trap. For they have been held captive by him to do whatever he wants.

Quality vs Sanctity of Life
ABORTION

CHAPTER 7

DEFINITION

a·bor·tion (ə-bôr'shən) *noun.*

1. *Medical*
   a. Termination of pregnancy and expulsion of an embryo or of a fetus that is incapable of survival.
   b. Any of various procedures that result in such termination and expulsion. Also called **induced abortion**.
2. The premature expulsion of a nonviable fetus from the uterus; a miscarriage.

   Dictionary.com from The American Heritage® Dictionary of the English Language, Fourth Edition copyright ©2000 by Houghton Mifflin Company.

AN OVERVIEW OF ABORTION IN THE UNITED STATES

Developed by Physicians for Reproductive Choice and Health® (PRCH) and The Alan Guttmacher Institute (AGI) © January 2003

Unintended Pregnancies
(Approximately 3.0 Million Annually)

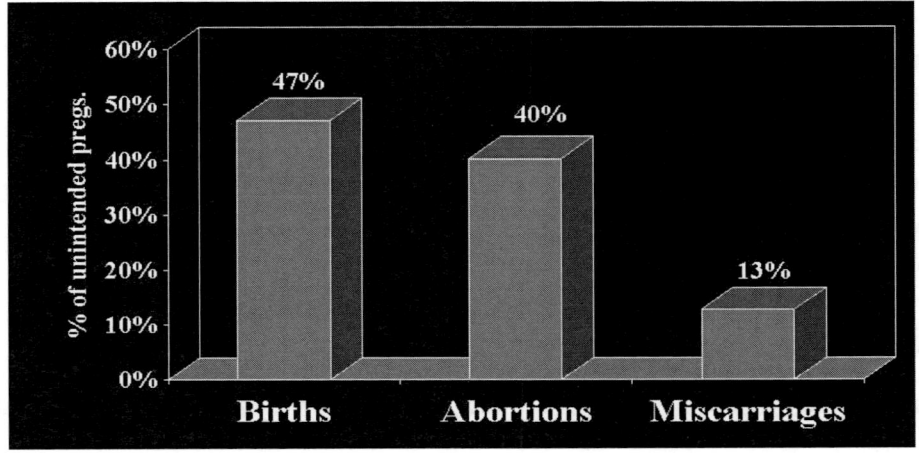

ABORTION IN THE UNITED STATES: STATISTICS & TRENDS

Each year, about 1.3 million pregnancies are terminated by abortion in the United States.

Abortion is one of the most common surgical procedures in the United States.

By age 20, 1 in 7 women have had at least one abortion; by age 45, 4 in 10 have done so.

Annual Number of Abortions Per 1,000 Women Aged 15–44

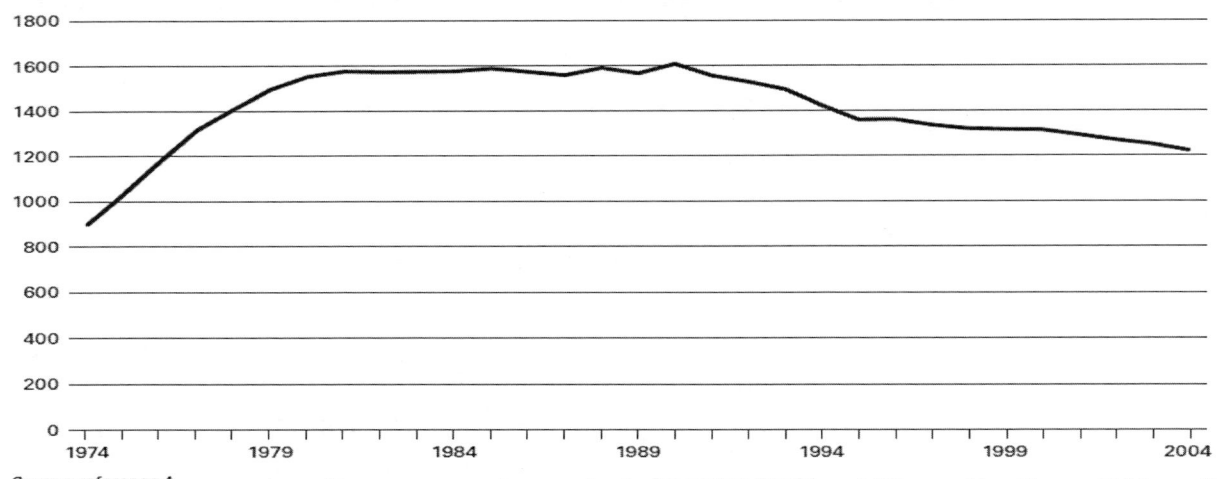

FIGURE 1. Annual number of abortions (in 000s) in selected years, 1974–2004

Source: reference 4.   http://www.guttmacher.org/pubs/2008/09/23/TrendsWomenAbortions-wTables.pdf

The Consequences of *Roe v. Wade*

— —,— — —,— — —

Total Abortions since 1973

Most Important Reasons Given for Terminating an Unwanted Pregnancy_____ _____%

2. Not ready for _____ ...._____%

3. Woman's life would be changed too much ...._____%

4. Problems with _____, _____..............................._____%

5. ..._____ ...._____%

6. Fetus has possible health problem..._____%

7. Woman has health problem..._____%

8. Pregnancy caused by _____ or _____..............................._____%

9. Other.._____%

10. Average number of reasons given..._____%

OPERATIONAL DEFINITION

ABORTION: the deliberate termination of a human being from the moment of conception until just prior to birth. This term is often made to sound innocuous. However, in an abortion, not only is the pregnancy or the product of conception terminated, so is a human.

ABORTION: A LEGAL HISTORY IN THE UNITED STATES

A. Prior to Roe V. Wade, most states made abortion a crime except for saving the mother.

B. Legal cases that led to Roe V. Wade

    1. _____ v. _____   Decided June 7, 1965

    2. _____ v. _____   Decided March 22, 1972

C. Roe v. Wade – Jan. 22, 1973

    1. Situation: Jane Roe (Norma McCorvey) -

    2. Main Ruling - Lifted bans on abortion in all 50 states A woman's "right to privacy" extends to her liberty to terminate an unwanted pregnancy.

    3. What the Supreme Court declared:

- "The Constitution does not define 'person'…"
- "person" has "application only post-natal"
- "The word 'person' as used in the Fourteenth Amendment, does not include the unborn."

IV Amendment to the U.S. Constitution

"The right of the people to be secure in their persons, houses, papers, and effects, against unreasonable searches and seizures, shall not be violated, …"

Amendment XIV Section 1 to the U.S. Constitution

All persons born or naturalized in the United States, and subject to the jurisdiction thereof, are citizens of the United States… nor shall any State deprive any person of life, liberty, or property, without due process of law; nor deny to any person within its jurisdiction the equal protection of the laws.

> **The unborn are essentially non-persons and do not fall under the protection of the 4th or 14th Amendments.**

KEY LEGAL CASES

1. _____ v _____ – Jan. 22, 1973

   Main Ruling - Lifted bans on abortion in all 50 states A woman's "right to privacy" extends to her liberty to terminate an unwanted pregnancy.

2. _____ v _____ – Jan. 22, 1973

   Main Ruling - Expanded definition of "health" of the mother to include familial, financial, psychological, well-being, etc. as determined by her physician.

3. _____ _____ v _____ – 1992

   Main Ruling - Discarded 3rd trimester of Roe and focused on the "viability" of the fetus as the determining point where a state's interest in unborn life begins.

4. _____ - _____ abortion ban act – 2003

   WASHINGTON, D.C. -- *President Bush signed the Partial-Birth Abortion Ban Act (S. 3) into law on November 5, 2003, The bill represents the first direct national restriction on any method of abortion since the Supreme Court legalized abortion on demand in 1973.*

TYPES OF ABORTION

A. Saline Injection.

- Amniotic fluid is removed and replaced with a toxic saline solution
- Baby ingest the toxins and dies 1-2 hours later from salt poisoning, dehydration, and hemorrhaging
- 24 hours later the mother goes into labor delivering a dead baby
- Chemical burning of the skin causes a painful death for the baby

B. Hysteronomy.

- Used in last trimester
- Baby removed as in a Cesarean birth
- Baby set aside and allowed to die or killed by a deliberate act

C. Suction & Aspiration.

- Used on 80% of abortions up to 12th week of pregnancy
- Hollow tube with knifelike edged tip is inserted into the womb
- A suction machine with force 28 times greater than a vacuum cleaner literally rips the developing baby to pieces and sucks the remains into a container to be disposed

D. Dilation and Curettage.

- Dilate cervix to allow the insertion of curetta—a loop-shaped knife—into the womb.
- Instrument scrapes placenta from the uterus and cuts baby apart; pieces are drawn through the cervix.
- Baby is re-assembled to be sure that all parts are accounted for
- If parts are left inside, the mother could bleed or become infected

E. Dilation and Evacuation.

- Used between 12 and 24 weeks
- The child is cut to pieces by a sharp knife, as in D & C
- The child is much larger and far more developed
- The child weighs as much as a pound and is as much as a foot in length

F. Prostaglandin.

- Prostaglandin hormones are injected into womb or released in
- Vaginal suppository cause uterus to contract and deliver baby prematurely
- Sometimes a saline solution is used to kill baby before the premature birth

G. RU 486

- Synthetic steroid used 5-7 weeks after conception
- Deprives baby of vital nutritional hormone progesterone
- Child starves to death as nutrient lining of the womb sloughs off
- Delivery of a dead baby

H. Partial-birth abortion

- The baby's leg is pulled out into the birth canal
- The abortionist delivers the baby's body, except for the head
- The abortionist jams scissors into the baby's skull. The scissors are then opened to enlarge the skull
- The scissors are removed and a suction catheter is inserted. The child's brains are evacuated out, causing the skull to collapse. The dead baby is then removed.

Note: I - K could be argued as abortive when one believes that life begins at conception

I. Intrauterine Device (IUD)

- The intrauterine device (IUD) is a long-term birth control method. Unlike IUDs that were used in the 1970s, present-day IUDs are small, safe, and highly effective. An IUD is a small, T-shaped plastic device that is wrapped in copper or contains hormones. The IUD is inserted into your uterus by your doctor.
- An IUD prevents fertilization of the egg by damaging or killing sperm. The IUD also affects the uterine lining (where a fertilized egg would implant and grow).

J. Morning after pill

- High-powered birth control pill

K. Birth control pill

- Stage 1 -Prevent ovulation
- Stage 2 -Stop conception by thickening cervical mucus
- Stage 3 -Stop implantation – by thinning the uterine wall

KEY QUESTION: WHEN DOES (A NEW) LIFE BEGIN?

- _____?
- _____?
- _____ _____?
- _____?
- _____ _____?
- _____?
- _____ development?

ARGUMENTS: NEW LIFE BEGINS AT CONCEPTION

A. Arguments from **SCIENCE**

"Many people mistakenly feel that abortion is a "religious" issue. But it is not. It is a scientific issue, and specifically, a biological issue."

(http://www.johnankerberg.org/Articles/apologetics/AP0805W3.htm)

Dr. Keith L. Moore, Professor and Chairman of the Department of Anatomy, University of Toronto - Essentials of Human Embryology states:

"Human development is a continuous process that begins when an ovum from a female is fertilized by a sperm from a male. Growth and differentiation transform the zygote, a single cell... into a multi-celled adult human being."

textbook on human embryology)

Professor Micheline Matthews-Roth, Harvard University Medical School:

"In biology and in medicine, it is an accepted fact that the life of any individual organism, reproducing by sexual production, begins at conception."

(http://topics.nytimes.com/top/reference/timestopics/subjects/a/abortion/index.html?s=oldest&off-set=70&inline=nyt-classifier)

B. Arguments from the **SCRIPTURES**

- The _____ are known by God (Jer. 1:5; Ps. 139:13; Job 31:15)
- The life of the unborn is _____ by the same punishment for injury or death as that of an adult (Ex 21:22-23)
- Christ was human from the point of conception (Matt 1:18, Luke 1:35)
- Unborn children possess _____ characteristics such as sin (Ps. 51:5) and joy (Lk 1:41,44) that are distinctive of persons

A HELPING STRATEGY
The Woman considering an abortion.

Taken from: The Billy Graham Workers Handbook. A copy of the entire handbook can be downloaded free in as a pdf file from: http://www.needhimresources.com/webtraining/documents/Billy_Graham_Handbook.pdf

- Commend her for calling.
- Tactfully remind her that she quite possibly has strong feelings about the moral implications of abortion or she wouldn't have called.
- Avoid being judgmental about her situation.
- Question her about her feelings on abortion:
  - ✓ What promoted you to call about your problem?
  - ✓ What are your real feelings about abortion?
  - ✓ What have you heard from others, Christian or not regarding abortion?
- Whether or not she believes abortion is wrong, present the Scriptures given in class along with any others that you think would apply.
- Ask her to consider the alternatives.
- If she is concerned about not being able to care for or support the child, ask her to consider adoption.
- Ask her if she has ever received Jesus Christ as her Lord and Savior. If appropriate, present the gospel.
- Suggest that she start reading the Bible.
- Ask if she has a church home. She should try to identify with a Bible-teaching church where she can find fellowship and encouragement, and can grow in her faith.

COUNSEL & CARE

The Woman who has had an Abortion and suffers from guilt.

- Encourage her by saying that she has made the right choice in seeking help. We care and want to help in any way we can. God has an answer to every human situation, and she can trust Him to work for her good.
- Don't make a moral issue of her situation; at the same time, don't minimize the seriousness of such a choice. The fact that she is willing to share her feelings of guilt is an indication that God is speaking to her.
- Dwell on God's forgiveness for those who are willing to repent and confess their sins to the Lord. To the woman taken in the act of adultery, Jesus said, "Neither do I condemn you; go and sin no more" (John 8: 11).
- Should confession result, do not dwell on the past (Philippians 3: 13-14).
- gospel.
- Suggest that she seek fellowship with God through Bible reading and prayer. Forgiveness is immediate, but a sense of restoration and acceptance will come in due time. Through commitment to this important discipline of prayer and Bible study, she will grow in her relationship with God.
- Suggest that she seek, or restore, fellowship with a Bible-teaching church. There she can counsel with a pastor, hear God's Word taught, and find strength through Christian relationships.
- Pray with her. Ask God for forgiveness, commitment, and strength for the future.

Selected Scriptures for Healing

Anger	Eph. 4:26, 31-32; Heb. 12:15
Depression	Psalm 40:1-5, 8-17; Psalm 6
Forgiveness	Psalm 32:1-5; Psalm 51:1-3; I John 1:9; 2 Cor. 5:21; Col 3:12-13
Peace	Col 3:15; Matt 11:28-30; Isa. 26:3-4;
Support	Gal 6:1-2; Psalm 27
Perseverance	Heb. 12:1-2; Gal 2:20; 1 Cor. 6:11; Phil 3:13-14

BIBLICAL WORLDVIEW & ABORTION

A look at Creation, Fall, Redemption

The greatest possible Being is _____

C

F

R

Psalms 139:13, 15

*For you formed my inward parts, you covered me **in my mother's womb**. My frame was not hidden from you when I was made in secret, and skillfully wrought in the lowest parts of the earth.*

Quality vs Sanctity of Life

EUTHANASIA

CHAPTER 8

DEFINITION

eu·tha·na·sia (y͞oo′thə-nā′zhə, -zhē-ə) **noun**

The act or practice of ending the life of an individual suffering from a terminal illness or an incurable condition, as by lethal injection or the suspension of extraordinary medical treatment.

Dictionary.com from The American Heritage® Dictionary of the English Language, Fourth Edition copyright ©2000 by Houghton Mifflin Company:

The term euthanasia is derived from the Greek prefix <u>eu</u>, meaning "good" or easy," and the Greek noun <u>thanatos</u>, meaning "death." Today the word is used to denote the act of one person killing another because the person killed is terminally ill, suffering, disabled, or elderly.

EUPHEMISMS

►

►

► "Compassion in Dying"

► "Planned Death"

►

TYPES OF EUTHANASIA

1. _____ Euthanasia

   Withholding medical treatment or discontinuing treatment ..."letting die"...cause of death is the same as the condition causing the suffering (disease, respiratory failure, etc).

2. _____ Euthanasia

   Actively doing something to bring about the death of the patient...lethal injection, smothering with a pillow, etc....the cause of death is not the condition causing the suffering, but rather something else.

3. _____ Euthanasia

   Patient does not request their own death - someone else decides for them that they are better off dead. Usually when a patient is unable to communicate (coma) or unable to understand their condition.

4. _____ Euthanasia

   Patient requests their own death - either verbally, in writing or via a living will. (Some states will recognize testimony of family/friends, but not all)

These types combine to give us 4 Basic Forms of Euthanasia

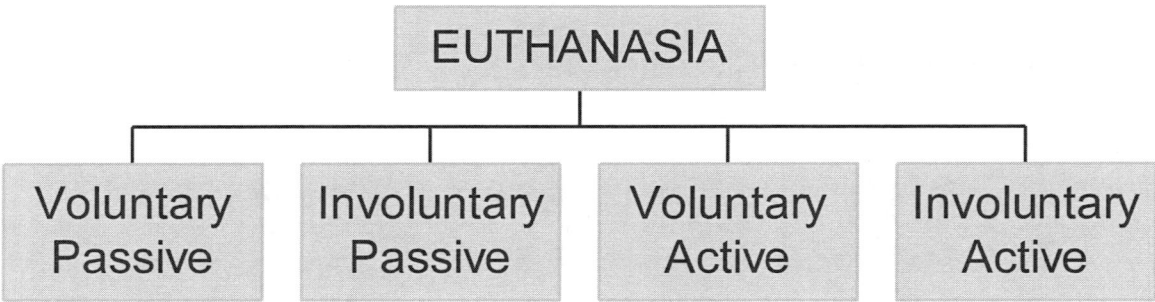

Physician-Assisted Suicide

This is a suicide in which a person's reasons for dying are similar to that of euthanasia. However, rather than take his or her own life, the person is assisted in the suicide by a physician.

PROMINENT NAMES TO KNOW

A. _____ – head of Hemlock Society

B. _____ – Dr. Death

C. _____ – persistent vegetative state, taken off life support in 1976 and lived 10 more years

D. _____ – suffered severe brain damage in 1990 and finally taken off life support and feeding tube in 2005 and died.

E. _____ – had terminal cancer and her doctor-assisted death stands out from other cases partially because she does not resemble the typical doctor-assisted suicide patient in Oregon, whose median age is 71.

F. _____ – 2017 Supreme Court Justice appointed by President Trump.

G. _____ – British courts order the doctors not to seek further treatment and to allow the baby to die

Dr. Kevorkian

> **QUOTATION**
>
> "...all human beings are intrinsically valuable and the intentional taking of human life by private persons is always wrong."
> The Future of Assisted Suicide and Euthanasia
> Neil M. Gorsuch

FIVE MAIN ARGUMENTS

▶

▶

▶

▶

▶

COMMONLY USED DEFENSE FOR EUTHANASIA

A.   It is a _____ issue

B.   Guidelines can prevent uses/abuses

C.   It would only be for the "_____ _____"

D.   We euthanize _____ to relieve suffering, why not

     people?

E.   There is no difference between "choice" in _____ and "choice" in
     euthanasia. True or False?

MEDICAL OPINIONS

American Medical Association-

British Medical Association-

World Medical Association-

CONSEQUENCES

A.   When life is devalued, it slowly depreciates further over time.

> **QUOTATION**
>
> Protecting from one end of the age spectrum to the other, we see euthanasia for the elderly as the counterpart to abortion for the very young. There is no moral distinction between the two. Quality-of-life proponent Joseph Fletcher agrees: 'To speak of living and dying, therefore... encompasses the abortion issue along with the euthanasia issue. They are ethically inseparable.' Those who take comfort in the fact that euthanasia is not practiced at present in America are leaning on a slim reed.
>
> **(Francis Schaeffer, The Great Evangelical Disaster, 1984)**

B.   _____ Ethic is replacing a _____ Ethic

C.   A _____ to die will eventually be transformed into a _____ to die

The power to _____ will broaden from the individual to the "caregivers" to those "financially invested" to "institutions" and so on.

D.   Options will become less available

E.   Expanding expendability is inevitable

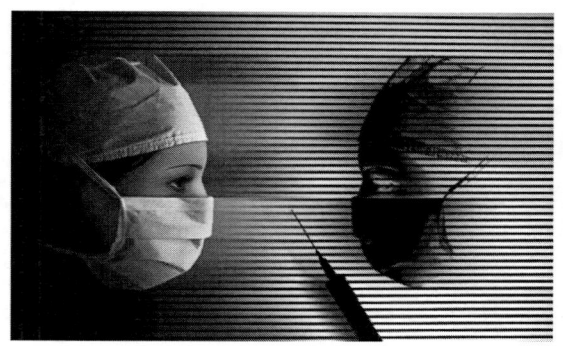

TRADITIONAL ARGUMENTS AGAINST EUTHANASIA

A.   _____

B.   Physician/Patient relationship will weaken

C.   _____ ethic leads to some lives being deemed more _____ than others.

D.   Abuses of the process & guidelines

E.   Diagnoses and prognoses may be _____

F.   There will become a _____

G.   Violation of the _____ _____

BIBLICAL VIEW OF EUTHANASIA

A.   Man is created in the _____ (Gen. 1:26)

B.   Human life is _____ and should not be terminated merely because it is difficult.

C.   God is sovereign over life and death. (Job 1:21; Deut. 32:39; Ps. 139:16)

D.   Bible specifically condemns the taking of life. (Ex. 20:13)

E.   Our body as well as our spirit belongs to God. (1 Co. 6:19-20)

F.   God has a purpose for everything even when we don't understand that purpose. (Rom. 8:28; 11:33)

G.   Suffering has a place in God's _____ (2 Cor. 1:8)

H.   As a result of the fall, _____ is inevitable (Rom. 5:12; 6:23)

HOSPICE INFORMATION: IS IT THE SAME?

A.   Help patients and families deal with the fear of the unknown

B.   Help with pain control

C.   Thoughts of suicide and depression are dealt with

D.   They deal with the "burden" issue

E.   They help the family deal with the care of the dying

WHAT CAN WE DO?

► Be Informed

   o   Inform _____

   o   Inform people of the dangers of "_____"

   o   Learn techniques in _____ management (Hospice has resources)

► Be Involved

► Be In Touch

Cultural Engagement

GENDER IDENTITY

CHAPTER 9

> "If male and female lose their meaning, then husband and wife lose their meaning. And then mom and dad loses its meaning."
>
> John Stonestreet

DEFINITION

Gender, *noun*
1. Sexuality identity, especially in relation to society or culture.
    a. The condition of being female or male; sex.
    b. Females or males considered as a group

Sex, *noun*
1. either the male or female division of a species, esp. as differentiated with reference to the reproductive functions.
2. the sum of the structural and functional differences by which the male and female are distinguished, or the phenomena or behavior dependent on these differences.
3. the instinct or attraction drawing one sex toward another, or its manifestation in life and conduct.

The American Heritage® Dictionary of the English Language, Fourth Edition copyright ©2000 by Houghton Mifflin Company:

C _____ -*It was good, very good.*

MALE & FEMALE ISSUES
The Trinity Conversation-"*Let us…*"   Gen. 1:26-27; 2:7, 15, 21-24

> **"The proper study of man begins with a proper study of God"** John Calvin

Image of God (a _____ type of being)

1. **Special:** Shared value apart from other creation (angels, animals, etc.), but with God:

   a. _____ Image speaks because God speaks.

   b. _____ Image thinks because God thinks.

   c. _____ Image wills because God wills.

   d. Aestheticism – Image appreciates beauty because God appreciates beauty.

   excerpts from James M. Grier, Christian Worldview Manual, 1999

2. **Reflect the Trinity** -- Male image of God & Female image of God were co-agents of creation.

   Be _____

   Live out _____ in _____

3. **Relationships**

   a. To _____

   b. To _____ Image

   c. To _____

F_____*-It was bad, very bad.*

Image is _____

Issues between Genders begin:

1. The _____ Game

2. The _____ Game

3. The _____ Game

4. The _____ Game

R_____*-It was very bad, yet very good again.*

- ► Restored a right relationship with _____.

- ► Restored a right relationship with fellow _____.

- ► Restored a right relationship with _____.

ROLES IN SOCIETY

1. Leave a Mark -- Gen. 2:15, 23
2. Subdue and rule over everything on the earth – Gen. 1:28
3. Use Spiritual gifts. – Rom 12; 1 Cor. 12
4. Spiritual equality in Christ – Galatians 3:28
5. Business leaders in the community. – Prov. 31:10-31
    - ► There is NO reason why a woman cannot be a CEO etc...
    - ► There is NO reason why women shouldn't receive equal pay.

ROLES IN THE HOME

1. The husband

- **Love his wife and sacrifice for her.**   **Eph. 5:25; Col. 3:19**
- **Head of the wife.**   **Eph. 5:23,24; Titus 2:5, I Cor. 11:3**
- **Provide for his family.**   **I Tim. 5:8**
- **Honor and respect wife.**   **I Peter 3:7**
- **Provide a positive environment for children.**   **Col. 3:21**

2. The wife

- **Submit to her husband, (not to men in general). Eph. 5:22-24; I Peter 3:1-6, 2 Cor. 11:3**

> The principle of subordination and authority pervades the entire universe. Paul shows that woman's subordination to man is but a reflection of that greater general truth. Christ is the head of every man, and the man is the head of a woman, and God is the head of Christ. If Christ had not submitted to the will of God, redemption for mankind would have been impossible, and we would forever be doomed and lost. If individual human beings do not submit to Christ as Savior and Lord, they are still doomed and lost, because they reject God's gracious provision. And if women do not submit to men, then the family and society

MacArthur, John F., 1 Corinthians: The MacArthur New Testament Commentary,(Chicago: Moody Press) 1984

- **Respect her husband**   **Eph. 5:33**
- **Love her children**   **Titus 2:4**
- **Keep her family a priority.**   **Titus 2:5; 2 Timothy 5:14**

ROLES IN THE CHURCH

1. Male Roles

2. Female Roles

- **Train younger women**   **Titus 2:3-4**
- **Teach children**   **2 Tim. 1:5, 3:15**
- **Pray**   **2 Cor 11:5**
- **Sing**   **Col. 3:16** (nothing gender specific. Note v. 18)
- **Correct false teaching**   **Acts 18:26 (Aquila, Priscilla & Apollos)**

- ▶ Vote Acts 1:14-26 (Women took part in voting for a replacement for Judas Iscariot)
- ▶ Serve as Deaconess   Rom. 16:1, 2 (Pheobe)
- ▶ Serve under the Senior Pastor   I Tim. 2:11-14, 3:1-2

NOTE: The issue with the role of women is not about ability or value, it is about authority, as given by God, not man.

GENDER IDENTITY

UNDERSTANDING THE "NEW" GENDER LANGUAGE

Note: The following definitions represent how the larger public is viewing these matters regarding sexual orientation and gender, and do not necessarily reflect your professor's or this institution's understanding of sex and gender).

Defining Terms

LGBTQ

lesbian, gay, bisexual, transgender, queer, or questioning.

Sexual Orientation

Describes which gender identities you are attracted to sexually and/or romantically.

http://www.acpeds.org/the-college-speaks/position-statements/gender-ideology-harms-children

SEX VS. GENDER

Many people think that sex and gender are pretty much the same, but there is actually a big difference.

Sex is biological

It is about the body. It includes an understanding of genes, hormones, and physical parts (like genitals) that people use to determine if the bodies are female, male, or intersex (people whose bodies are not clearly female or male).

Gender

It is how society thinks a person should look, think, and act as girls and boys, women, and men.

Gender identity

It is how a person feels about sex and gender.

Gender expression

It is a person's communication about their sense of being masculine, feminine or androgynous. This may or may not be related to a person's gender identity. It is expressed by the way they dress, act, speak, etc.

Trans

It can include people who do not identify with the strict male/female gender roles the world tells us people fit into. Sometimes people who do not feel either male or female call themselves genderqueer or just queer or questioning.

TRANSGENDER VS. TRANSSEXUAL

Transgender

The "T" in LGBTQ. Some people have a gender identity that doesn't match up with their biological sex — for example, they were born with "female" sex organs (vulva, vagina, uterus), but they feel like a male. People in this community sometimes call themselves transgender or trans. (Don't use terms like transgendered, tranny, or, he-she — they're old-fashioned and hurtful).

- ✓ It's used as the umbrella term for the transgender and transsexual community.
- ✓ Specifically defined as anyone whose gender expression (communication of gender) is considered non-traditional for the sex they were assigned at birth, such as transsexuals, cross dressers, drag artists, androgynous individuals, genderqueers, masculine women, feminine men and other gender variant individuals.

Transsexual

- ✓ A person who identifies psychologically as one gender/sex other than the one to which they were assigned at birth.
- ✓ To match their outer body to their inner sense of gender/sex, a transsexual person may change or have changed their body through hormone therapy and gender confirmation surgeries.

  Source for above definitions: All About LGBTQ at a Glance (Based off of Planned Parenthood's Website https://www.plannedparenthood.org/teens/lgbtq/all-about-lgbtq

IMPORTANT TERMS

Intersexual (*formerly known as Hermaphrodite*)

- ✓ Many cases of intersexuality have their origin in utero and involve varying degrees of what is called Androgen Insensitivity Syndrome (AIS).

- ✓ This insensitivity to androgen – a male sex hormone – can interfere in the normal development of the sex organs and result in ambiguous genitalia as described above. http://www.pureintimacy.org/w/what-is-intersexuality-and-how-should-christians-respond/

Gender Dysphoria

Gender identity is simply how people experience themselves as male or female, including how masculine or feminine they feel.

Gender dysphoria refers to deep and abiding discomfort over the incongruence between one's biological sex and one's psychological and emotional experience of gender.

Contemporary Gender Analysis

Bi-Gender: A Lesson In Gender Identity

Etymological analysis of the term. Notice that "gender" is seen as originally synonymous with "sex."

GENDER (From the online etymology dictionary)

http://www.etymonline.com/index.php?allowed_in_frame=0&search=gender)

c.1300, from O.Fr. gendre, from stem of L. genus (gen. generis) "kind, sort, gender," also "sex"; As sex took on erotic qualities in 20c., gender came to be used for "sex of a human being," . . . in feminist writing with reference to social attributes as much as biological qualities; this sense first attested 1963.

✓ Gender-bender is first attested 1980, with reference to pop star David Bowie.

✓ Trans gender - by 1988, from trans + gender.

Note: the split between "sex" and "gender" is a new development. Historically, the two terms have been synonymous.

Prominent Names

RuPaul

Andre Charles (born November 17, 1960), best known mononymously as RuPaul, is an American actor, drag queen, model, author, and recording artist.

"When you become the image of your own imagination, it's the most powerful thing you could ever do." RuPaul (http://www.dragofficial.com/ali/25-rupaul-quotes-to-live-by)

Bruce Jenner

Caitlyn Marie Jenner", formerly known as "Bruce Jenner", is an American television personality and retired Olympic gold medal-winning decathlete.

April 24th, 2015 in an interview with Dianne Sawyer, Jenner states, "Yes, for all intents and purposes I am a woman."

Pat Cordova (see notes under Legal Cases or Ramifications)

Key Legal Cases

New York: Maffei v. Kolaeton Industries, Inc.

A state court in New York City finds that the New York City Human Right Law's prohibition against "gender" discrimination applies to a transsexual man. 1995. http://www.transgenderlaw.org/cases/maffei.htm

Florida: In Smith v. Jacksonville Correctional Institution *October 2, 1991,*

The Division of Administrative Hearings held that an individual with gender dysphoria is protected by Florida Human Rights Act's prohibitions of discrimination based on disability and perceived disability. (Underlined emphasis added) http://www.transgenderlaw.org/cases/

California: Assembly Bill No. 1266

CHAPTER 85

An act to amend Section 221.5 of the Education Code, relating to pupil rights.

A 17 year old California high school student, Pat Cordova-Goff who believes he is trapped in a boy's body has been allowed to join the girls' softball team.

Colorado:

Girl Scouts of Colorado (An example of a Non-Profit organization)

Girl scouts allow a 7 year old boy to join because he is living life as a girl.

http://www.cnsnews.com/news/article/girl-scouts-allow-7-year-old-boy-join-because-he-living-life-girl

NCAA

"Policy development governing the inclusion of transgender student-athletes is an emerging endeavor. As new research on the participation of transgender athletes and the physiological effects of gender transition on athletic performance becomes available, policies may need to be re-evaluated to ensure that they reflect the most current research-based information."

https://www.ncaa.org/sites/default/files/Transgender_Handbook_2011_Final.pdf

North Carolina HB2

The Public Facilities Privacy & Security Act, officially called An Act to Provide for Single-sex Multiple Occupancy Bathroom and Changing Facilities in Schools and Public Agencies and to Create Statewide Consistency in Regulation of Employment and Public Accommodations but commonly known as House Bill 2 or HB2.

https://en.wikipedia.org/wiki/Public_Facilities_Privacy_%26_Security_Act

A BIBLICAL PERSPECTIVE & DEFINING OF GENDER

The Bible records God creative order as seen in Male & Female.

Genesis 1:26-27 (NIV) - (26) "Then God said, 'Let us make human beings in our image, to be like us. They will reign over the fish in the sea, the birds in the sky, the livestock, all the wild animals on the earth, and the small animals that scurry along the ground.'(27) So God created human beings in his own image. In the image of God he created them; male and female he created them."

Jesus addresses gender in Matthew 19:4 - "Haven't you read," he replied, "that at the beginning the Creator 'made them male and female,'"

Gender distinctions are obviously important to God –Deut. 22:5, Rom. 1:24-25, 1 Cor. 11:1-16.

Humans (Male & Female) are "broken" as a result of the Fall (Genesis 3)

Numerous passages emphasize the pervasiveness of our fallenness/brokenness (Gen. 6:5, 8:21, Ps. 51:5, Jer. 19:9, Rom. 7:15-24 (but don't forget v. 25)

God has called the church to love our transgender neighbors. (Matthew 22:39)

God has called the church to evangelize/disciple the world. (Matthew 28:19-20)

God has called the church to "speak the truth in love" with our brothers and sisters in Christ (Ephesians 4:15).

QUOTATION

The givenness of maleness and femaleness has of course been impacted by the fall, [...]. Thus, there are now on occasion gender anomalies in nature, and there is sometimes sexual confusion with the psyche of an individual. But anomalies and confusions in the fallen world do not negate the normative structure of God's designs. This givenness is the standard toward which we are to orient all sexual expression and the context in which all sexual behavior is to be experienced.

Hollinger, (2009) *The Meaning of Sex* **(p. 77)**

THREE CULTURAL LENSES (DR. MARK YARHOUSE)

Lens #1: Integrity.

The integrity lens views sex and gender and, therefore, gender identity in terms of what theologian Robert Gagnon refers to as "the sacred integrity of maleness or femaleness stamped on one's body."

Lens #2: Disability.

This lens views gender dysphoria as a result of living in a fallen world, but not a direct result of moral choice.

Lens #3: Diversity.

This lens sees the reality of transgender persons as something to be celebrated, honored, or revered. Our society is rapidly moving in this direction.

Cultural Engagement
HOMOSEXUALITY
CHAPTER 10

DEFINITION

ho·mo·sex·u·al·i·ty (hō′mə-sĕk′shōō-ăl′ĭ-tē, -mō-) *noun.*

1. Sexual orientation to persons of the same gender.
2. Sexual activity with another of the same gender.

Dictionary.com from The American Heritage® Dictionary of the English Language, Fourth Edition copyright ©2000 by Houghton Mifflin Company:

BIBLICAL INFORMATION

Homosexuality was considered a sin in the days of the _____.

1. Gen 18:20 "their sin is very grievous"

2. Gen 19:1-12 Sodom and Gomorrah

3. cross reference: Jude 7

Homosexuality was considered a "capital crime" in the _____ Law.

1. Lev. 18:22 "abomination" or "detestable"

2. Lev. 20:13

3. Note: _____

The _____ is clear in its condemnation of homosexual conduct.

1. I Cor. 6:9-10

2. Rom. 1:24-32

HOMOSEXUAL VIEW

The sin of Sodom was not homosexuality but inhospitality. This is due to the interpretation of Yada. Gen. 19:5

Some believe David and Jonathan were gay lovers. I Samuel 18-20; key verses 18:3, 4 20:41(KJV)

I Cor. 6:9 only speaks against offenses i.e. improper homosexual activity.

MYTHS BEHIND THE HOMOSEXUAL AGENDA

Homosexuality qualifies for minority status and special legal protection.

1. **MINORITY STATUS** - (To achieve minority status, a group must fulfill three requirements, none of which are met by homosexuals.)

This is the logo used by "Soulforce" an organization whose purpose is to promote the acceptance of the homosexual lifestyle.

   a. Inability to succeed

      1) *Response:* 49% hold professional, high-paying jobs; the average annual income for homosexual households is over $55,000.

   b. Immutable (unchangeable) Characteristics

      Response: They have no visible immutable characteristics such as skin color or gender.

2. **POLITICAL POWERLESSNESS**

   a. *Response:* They have not been denied the right to vote, access to public buildings, and restrooms, nor been legally segregated.

   b. They have always exercised and independently funded powerful political campaigns and causes.

Homosexuals compose 10% of the population.

1. *Response:* This figure based on the now discredited Kinsey sex studies of 1948-1952. Even homosexual leaders have recognized this but still use it in their propaganda for recruitment.

2. *Response:* Later, more objective studies indicated that only 1% - 3% were homosexual.

Homosexuality is genetically determined, thus uncontrollable

1. *Response:* Although several studies have indicated that this may be the case, the fact still remains that there is no conclusive scientific evidence that this is true.

2. *Response:* Converted homosexuals invariably say that this lifestyle they led was a personal choice. Even some homosexuals are not going for the genetic determinism argument.

3. *Response:* Alcoholism and violent tendencies may be inherited traits, but this does not make discrimination against these acts wrong.

Homosexuals cannot change

1. *Response:* There are too many former homosexuals who testify that they learned and then unlearned this behavior, while in it they were convinced they could not help themselves.

2. Organizations for helping people change through the power of Christ.
   c. Organizations Ministering to Homosexuals

   d. Exodus International: (CA) 415-454-1017

   e. Homosexuals Anonymous: (PA) 215-376-1146

   f. New Creation Ministries: (CA) 209-264-6125

   g. Regeneration (MD) 401-661-0284

The homosexual lifestyle is happy, healthy and responsible

1. *Response:* AIDS is most prevalent among gay men and is rising rapidly among lesbians.

2. *Response:* Monogamy among homosexuals is the exception, not the norm. It is a

compulsive lifestyle involving many sexual partners throughout their lifetime.

3. *Response:* The average gay has multiple sex partners during their gay life many of which are anonymous encounters in bathhouses, night clubs, and porn shops.

4. *Response:* The median age of death for homosexuals without AIDS is 42.

5. *Response:* The majority of homosexuals engage in sexual practices inherently conducive to serious illness and injury. Anal sex (sodomy) is inherently unhealthy and unsafe.

6. *Response:* Former homosexuals readily admit that their lives were characterized by loneliness, fear, depression and suicidal ideations and attempts.

7. *Response:* Independent studies show that only about 9% of homosexuals live to the age of 65, while the average life span for males is 75.

(Howe, Richard., Homosexuality in America: Exposing the Myths.
http://www.afa.net/homosexual_agenda/homosexuality.pdf)

A CHRISTIAN APPROACH TO HOMOSEXUALITY

▶ Speak the _____ in _____

"speaking the truth in love" (Eph 4:15).

And a servant of the Lord must not quarrel but be gentle to all, able to teach, patient, in humility correcting those who are in opposition, if God perhaps will grant them repentance, so that they may know the truth, and that they may come to their senses and escape the snare of the devil, having been taken captive by him to do his will. (2 Ti 2:24-26)

▶ Homosexuality is a _____ pattern that can be _____.
Do not be deceived: Neither the sexually immoral nor idolaters nor adulterers nor male prostitutes nor homosexual offenders... will inherit the kingdom of God. And that is what some of you were. But you were washed, you were sanctified, you were justified in the name of the Lord Jesus Christ and by the Spirit of our God. (I Cor. 6:9-11)

▶ _____ those who want to _____ homosexuality
Brethren, if a man is overtaken in any trespass, you who are spiritual restore such a one in a spirit of gentleness, considering yourself lest you also be tempted. Bear one another's burdens, and so fulfill the law of Christ. (Gal 6:1-2)

FIGURE 1

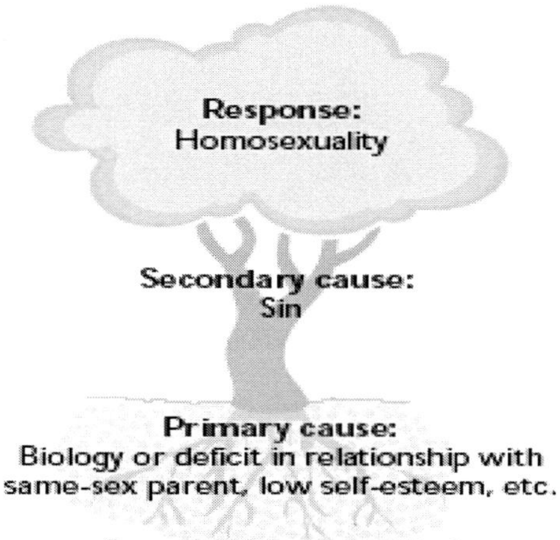

FIGURE 2

Response:
Homosexuality

Secondary cause:
Sin

Primary cause:
Biology or deficit in relationship with
same-sex parent, low self-esteem, etc.

**Common though unbiblical
conceptualization of the development of
homosexuality**

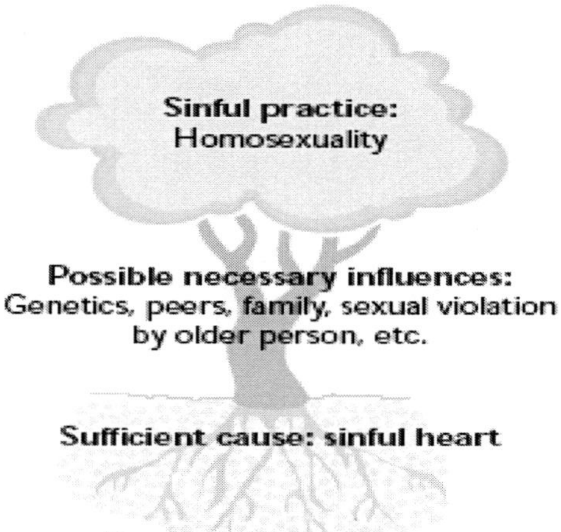

Sinful practice:
Homosexuality

Possible necessary influences:
Genetics, peers, family, sexual violation
by older person, etc.

Sufficient cause: sinful heart

**Biblical conceptualization
of the development of homosexuality**

Welch, Edward. Homosexuality: Current Thinking and Biblical Guidelines.
http://www.afa.net/homosexual_agenda/homosup.pdf)

WHAT SHOULD BE MY ATTITUDE TOWARD HOMOSEXUALITY?
(Taken from: The Moral Catastrophe by David Hocking)

Do not hate homosexuals; hate homosexuality and what it does to people.

Never believe that "sexual preferences" should be added to our understanding and application of human rights or civil rights.

Do not discriminate against homosexuals in terms of the rights to which all Americans are entitled, but never be intimidated or pressured to approve or accept their lifestyle and activity.

Teach your children what the Bible says about sexual matters, and warn them of sexual sins (adultery, homosexuality etc)

Do not treat homosexuality as a more terrible sin than adultery among heterosexuals, but never view it as harmless or tolerable.

Encourage homosexuals to accept God's love and forgiveness in the work and person of Jesus Christ. Show them that God's power can give them the inner strength, courage, and desire not to be involved in homosexual activities.

Make sure that your own personal beliefs, principles and lifestyle are in line with biblical morality. You should be committed to demonstrating that the only safe and right sex is between a husband and a wife.

THE BIBLICAL WORLDVIEW & HOMOSEXUALITY
Genesis 1-11

Leviticus 18:22 (NLT) - *"Do not practice homosexuality; it is a detestable sin.*

Romans 1:26-27 (KJV) *For this cause God gave them up unto vile affections: for even their women did change the natural use into that which is against nature: And likewise also the men, leaving the natural use of the woman, burned in their lust one toward another; men with men working that which is unseemly, and receiving in themselves that recompense of their error which was meet.*

Cultural Engagement

RELATIONSHIPS

CHAPTER 11

Marriage & Divorce

DEFINITION

mar·riage (măr′ĭj) *noun.*

a. The legal union of a man and woman as husband and wife.
b. The state of being married; wedlock.
c. A common-law marriage.
d. A union between two persons having the customary but usually not the legal force of marriage: *a same-sex marriage.*

Dictionary.com from The American Heritage® Dictionary of the English Language, Fourth Edition copyright ©2000 by Houghton Mifflin Company:

BIBLICAL INFORMATION ON MARRIAGE

A. Marriage is between a male and a female. Gen. 1:27-28; 2:21-24; Matt.19:4-5

B. Marriage involves a _____.   1 Cor. 7:2-4

C. Marriage involves a _____ before God.   Matthew 19:6

> "So they are no longer two, but one. Therefore what God has joined together, let man not separate."

D. God is a _____ of weddings, whether invited or not.   Matthew 19:6

E. Husband and wife are literally _____ together by God.　　　Matthew 19:6

F. Marriage is a _____ - _____ institution for all people. It is the only social institution ordained by God before the fall of mankind.　　　Genesis 2:24-25

FOUR ELEMENTS OF COMMITMENT

There is only one statement about marriage that God includes four times in the Scriptures. (Gen 2:24-25, Matt 19:5, Mark 10:7-8, Eph 5:31)

Therefore shall a man <u>leave</u> his father and his mother, and shall <u>cleave</u> unto his wife: and they <u>shall be one</u> flesh.

The Law of _____

A. "_____" – your parents

　　1. What it does **NOT** mean

　　　　a. That you totally forsake your parents　　　(Ex 21:17, Mk 7:9-11, I Tim 5:4-8)

　　　　b. That you must move 1000's of miles away. (It is possible to live two doors down and "leave", but it is also possible to be miles away and yet not "leave.")

　　2. What it does mean

　　　　a. Establish an adult _____ with them.

　　　　b. You are more concerned about your _____ ideas and approval.

　　　　c. It means that you do not "run" to mom and dad every time you have a problem.

　　　　d. You make the husband/wife relationship your _____ in human relationships.

The Law of _____

B. "_____" – to your spouse

　　1. Dict: _____

　　2. Society tells us that if it doesn't work to your _____ then simply get out!

3. God planned for marriage to last a _____. Mark 10:7-9

4. Cleaving until "death do us part"

The Law of _____

C. "_____" – one flesh

1. At its most elementary level this does refer to the sexual or physical union. (I Cor 6:16)

2. It means more than just the marriage act! In a marriage relationship we share everything.

   a. _____

   b. _____

   c. _____

   d. _____

The Law of _____

D. "_____" – no shame

1. Healthy nakedness must happen in a special place with the right person.

2. Sin is the greatest obstacle to openness.

3. Purity must be upheld by both partners to provide a climate for total exposure.

4. Nakedness was written about to show the original purity of mankind and of marriage.

7 KEYS TO A SUCCESSFUL MARRIAGE

1. _____   Start with Christ at the center of your relationship.

2. _____   To each other "till death do us part"

3. _____   Honest and open.

4. _____   Caring, considerate, working together as a team. As ONE flesh!

5. _____   They will come so handle them with grace. Build don't tear down!

6. _____   Yes...the sexual element is also important.

7. _____   Again, emphasize the spiritual growth in the relationship.

HUSBANDS & WIVES

Destructive Husbands

1. The _____ Husband

2. The _____ Husband

3. The _____ Husband

4. The _____ Husband

Destructive Wives

1. The _____ Wife

2. The _____ Wife

3. The _____ Wife

4. The _____ Wife

BIBLICAL MARRIAGE

God's
Responsibility

GOD
●

God
Needs

Man's
Responsibility

Man Needs ●

MAN

Woman's
Responsibility

● Woman Needs

WOMAN

DIVORCE

BIBLICAL INFORMATION ON DIVORCE

Deut. 24:1-4 --

Matt. 5:31-32 --

Matt. 19:1-8, Mark 10:2-12 –

1 Cor. 7 (especially v. 12ff) --

REASONS FOR THE INCREASED DIVORCE RATE

▶ **A rise in** _____: Concern has shifted from the well-being of families to personal happiness and success

▶ _____ **only lasts so long:** Society emphasizes a romantic love that can be replaced once the excitement is gone

▶ **Marriage is** _____: With both partners working (added stress)

▶ **Divorce is socially acceptable:** Society encourages couples to divorce (Attitude)

▶ **Legally a divorce is easy to obtain:** Couples can divorce simply by showing their marriage has failed (Opportunity)

▶ **Sexual** _____: Physically and emotionally (includes pornography)

▶ _____: More effort is put into getting things, than working on a marriage

> "In most states the classic grounds for divorce were cruelty, desertion, and adultery. This legal foundation changed when California enacted a statute in 1969 that allowed for no-fault divorce"
>
> Kirby Anderson, Moral Dilemmas, Word Publishers

A. Important Statistics - Kirby Anderson, Moral Dilemmas, Word Publishers

1. The divorce rate is around 13% not 50% as often stated.

2. Every year parents of over 1 million children divorce.

3. Divorce impacts children socially, educationally, emotionally, economically, and spiritually.

4. "Fundamental changes in our society in the last few decades have changed divorce from rare to routine."

5. "Marriage is no longer seen as a covenant; it is seen instead as a contract"

B. Christian Views on Divorce

1. Christian **AGREEMENT** on Divorce

    a. Divorce is not _____. Malachi 2:16; Matt. 19:6, 8

    b. Divorce is not permissible for every _____. Matt. 19:3, 9

    c. Divorce creates many problems.

2. Christian **DISAGREEMENT** on Divorce

    a. Some will say there are _____ _____ for divorce.

    ► Divorce violates God's design for marriage.

    ► Divorce breaks a vow made before God.

    ► Jesus condemned all divorce. Mk 10:1-9; Luke 16:18

    ► The apostle Paul condemned divorce. 1 Cor. 7:10-13

    ► Divorce disqualified an elder. 1 Timothy 3:2

    ► Divorce violates a sacred typology. Eph. 5:32 (God takes a violation of a sacred type seriously. See Numbers 20:9-12)

b. Others will contend that there is only _____ ground for divorce.

    ▶ Jesus mentions _____ as grounds for divorce. Matt. 19:9

    ▶ Jesus repeated this exception in a parallel passage. Matt. 5:32

c. Still others hold that there are _____ grounds for divorce.

    ▶ Paul approves of divorce for _____. 1 Cor. 7:15

    ▶ Even God "divorced" Israel for unfaithfulness. Jer. 3:8; Isaiah 50:1

    ▶ The Bible recognizes human frailty.

    ▶ Failing to allow divorce is legalistic. Mk 2:27

    ▶ Repentance changes the situation. There is only one unpardonable sin (Matt 12:32) and it is not divorce.

Cultural Engagement

RACISM

CHAPTER 12

DEFINITION

race (rā's) *noun.*

1. A group of persons related by common descent or heredity.

2. A population so related.

3. *Anthropology.*

   a. any of the traditional divisions of humankind, the commonest being the Caucasian, Mongoloid, and Negro, characterized by supposedly distinctive and universal physical characteristics: no longer in technical use.

   b. an arbitrary classification of modern humans, sometimes, esp. formerly, based on any or a combination of various physical characteristics, as skin color, facial form, or eye shape, and now frequently based on such genetic markers as blood groups.

   c. a human population partially isolated reproductively from other populations, whose members share a greater degree of physical and genetic similarity with one another than with other humans.

rac·ism (rā's ĭz' əm) *noun.*

1. The belief that race accounts for differences in human character or ability and that a particular race is superior to others.

2. Discrimination or prejudice based on race.

   Dictionary.com from The American Heritage® Dictionary of the English Language, Fourth Edition copyright ©2000 by Houghton Mifflin Company:

DEFINITION

Racism is…

The prejudice that members of one race are <u>intrinsically</u> <u>superior</u> to members of other races and include discriminatory or abusive behavior towards members of another race.

RACISM IS EVIDENCED BY:

A. _____ – A (usually negative) overgeneralization about a certain people group as a whole based on the unaccepted behavior of a few members of that group.

B. _____ – "Prejudging" an individual in a negative way because he/she happens to be from a stereotyped group.

C. _____ – Unequal treatment of a person on the basis of his/her people group membership.

D. _____ – Verbal and physical abuse directed toward people. This is considered justified on the basis of their group membership.

RACISM IS BASED ON:

A. **Irrational Beliefs** - That a certain people group as whole is intellectually or morally inferior.

B. **Pride (Ethnocentrism)** - Especially in inherited traits and culture (See 1 Corinthians 4:7).

   1. Ethnocentricity "is the tendency to look at the world primarily from the perspective of one's own ethnic culture".

   2. ETHNOCENTRISM [ethnocentrism] "the feeling that one's group has a mode of living, values, and patterns of adaptation that are superior to those of other groups. It is coupled with a generalized contempt for members of other groups. Ethnocentrism may manifest itself in attitudes of superiority or sometimes hostility. Violence, discrimination, proselytizing, and verbal aggressiveness are other means whereby ethnocentrism may be expressed"

C. **Ignorance**

   1. Educational

   The evolutionary view that life can evolve to "higher" levels provides fuel for racist ideas.

   The Bible on the other hand, clearly shows the fallacy of racism...this misleading concept gives rise to the idea that some "races" have developed and become more sophisticated faster than others, leading to the ultimate conclusion (often subconsciously) that certain "races" are superior   Creation Ex Nihilo 20 Dec 97

   2. Voluntary

D. **Fear**

    1. Of the unknown

    2. Of what is different

E. **Socialization**

    1. Parental example

    2. Uncritically accepted social assumptions

RACISM IS OPPOSED IN:

The Abrahamic Covenant –   Genesis 12:1-3, 15:5-6, Romans 4:17-18; Gal 3:26-29

The Mosaic Law –   Exodus 23:9

The Example of Jesus –   (The Samaritan Women at the well) John 4:1-10

The Teaching Jesus –   (Parable of the Good Samaritan) Luke 10:25-37

The Gospel as it breaks down divisive barriers and unifies races –
                Acts 15:7-9, Rom 1:14-16, I Cor. 12:13, Gal 3:28, Eph. 2:13-20, Col 3:10-15

Heaven will be a multicultural celebration of Christ!! –   Rev 5:9-10

HOW DOES OUR BIBLICAL WORLDVIEW CONFRONT THE RACISM ISSUE?

C_____ in that we are all _____

F_____ in that we are all _____

R_____ in that we are all _____

C_____ in that we are all _____

ONE BLOOD
Acts 17:26

Adam & Eve
1 Corinthians 15:45
Genesis 3:20

Sons & Daughters
Genesis 5:4

Noah & Sons
Genesis 9:17-19

People at Tower of Babel
Genesis 11:8-9

Different People Groups/Cultures

Graphic from: Answers in Genesis http://www.answersingenesis.org/docs2004/0209one_blood.asp

KEY ISSUES FOR THE CHURCH REGARDING RACISM:

A. *Interracial Marriage*

1. Marry _____   1 Cor. 7:39

2. What is a _____ marriage?
   Deuteronomy 7:3-4; Exodus 12:48-49; 2 Corinthians 6:14; Colossians 3:9-11

3. What are some questions to ask?

   - What are your cultural differences?

   - What do your families think about the marriage?

   - What are the consequences for your children?

4. Notice Numbers 12:1, 10.

5. What does the Bible say about the problems of interracial marriages?

B. *Racial* _____ *among believers*

    1. Why do believers of different races struggle to be in the same church together?

    2. Unity.

    3. Obstacles that block progress *(from Tony Evans – Can We Really Get Along? – an article taken from his book Let's Get To Know Each Other)*

       a. Our fear of losing our racial distinction

       b. Our cultural prejudice

       c. Our fear of the price tag of unity

       d. Our hesitancy to hold people accountable for racial prejudice

    4. Jesus' example in John 4

    5. Our priority - John 13:34-35; Luke 10:30-37; James 2:1-13

    6.

RACISM: CARE FOR OTHERS

Revelation 7:9

After this I looked, and there in front of me was a huge crowd of people. They stood in front of the throne and in front of the Lamb. There were so many that no one could count them. They came from **every nation, tribe, people and language.**

Redemption: Forgiveness

Healing & Holiness

SELF-REFLECTION

Examine your heart. Do you/have you devalued image?

Participate in a forgiveness service

Have conversations/dialogues

Cultural Engagement

POVERTY

CHAPTER 13

DEFINITION

pov·er·ty (pŏv′ər-tē) *noun.*

1. The state of being poor; lack of the means of providing material needs or comforts.
2. Deficiency in amount; scantiness: "the poverty of feeling that reduced her soul" (Scott Turow).
3. Unproductiveness; infertility: *the poverty of the soil.*
4. Renunciation made by a member of a religious order of the right to own property.

DEFINITION

poor (pŏŏr) *adj.* **poor·er, poor·est**

1. Having little or no wealth and few or no possessions.
2. Lacking in a specified resource or quality: *an area poor in timber and coal; a diet poor in calcium.*
3. Not adequate in quality; inferior: *a poor performance.*
4. *Quantity*
   a. Lacking in value; insufficient: *poor wages.*
   b. Lacking in quantity: *poor attendance.*
5. Lacking fertility: *poor soil.*
6. Undernourished; lean.
7. Humble: *a poor spirit.*
8. Eliciting or deserving pity; pitiable: *couldn't rescue the poor fellow.*

Dictionary.com from The American Heritage® Dictionary of the English Language, Fourth Edition copyright ©2000 by Houghton Mifflin Company:

HOW DO YOU DEFINE POOR?

CONNECTION: THE CHURCH & THE POOR

QUOTATION

DO WE REALLY KNOW our poor? Do we really know the poor in our own house, in our own family? Maybe we are not hungry for a piece of bread. Maybe our children, our husband, our wife, are not hungry, are not naked, are not homeless, but are you sure that there is no one there who feels, unwanted, unloved? Where are your old father and mother? Where are they?...Let us look straight into our own families, for love begins at home. Do we really understand the poverty of Christ, the poverty of our poor in our own home, in our own communities? Never turn your back to the poor. For in turning your back to the poor you are turning it to Jesus Christ.

Mother Teresa
1979 Franciscan Communications video Everyone, Everywhere

QUOTATION

I had come to see that the great tragedy in the church is not that rich Christians do not care about the poor but that rich Christians do not know the poor.
I truly believe that when the rich meet the poor, riches will have no meaning. And when the rich meet the poor, we will see poverty come to an end."

Shane Claiborne, The Irresistible Revolution:
Living as an Ordinary Radical

INFORMATION

The Best Ways to Fight Poverty: Ministries Respond Focus on Solving the Poverty of the Soul

Our aid to the poor should always address their area of greatest need.

Jesus said, "The poor you will always have with you" (Matt. 26:11). No matter how much food we give, how many shelters we provide, how many physicians we deploy or how much medicine we send, poverty remains. Does that mean that we should just shrug our shoulders and walk away? Of course not. Jesus never turned away from someone in need. Jesus did not come to give a better life, but to give eternal life. Every person Jesus helped, he did it in such a way that they would put their faith and trust in Him alone.

Franklin Graham, president of Samaritan's Purse 3/8/12 in Christianity Today

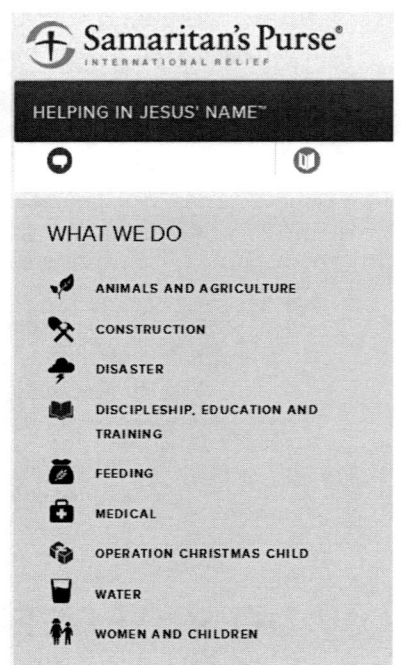

Samaritan's Purse®
INTERNATIONAL RELIEF

HELPING IN JESUS' NAME™

WHAT WE DO

- ANIMALS AND AGRICULTURE
- CONSTRUCTION
- DISASTER
- DISCIPLESHIP, EDUCATION AND TRAINING
- FEEDING
- MEDICAL
- OPERATION CHRISTMAS CHILD
- WATER
- WOMEN AND CHILDREN

POVERTY & THE POOR

Global Income

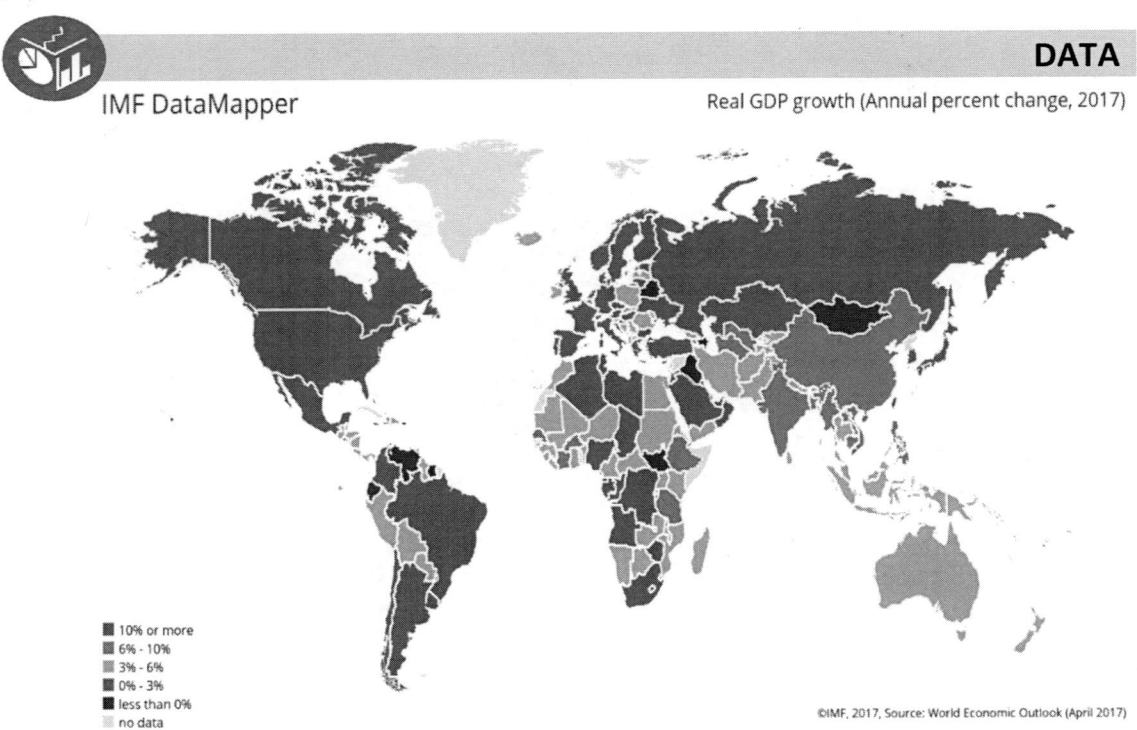

IMF DataMapper

DATA

Real GDP growth (Annual percent change, 2017)

- 10% or more
- 6% - 10%
- 3% - 6%
- 0% - 3%
- less than 0%
- no data

©IMF, 2017, Source: World Economic Outlook (April 2017)

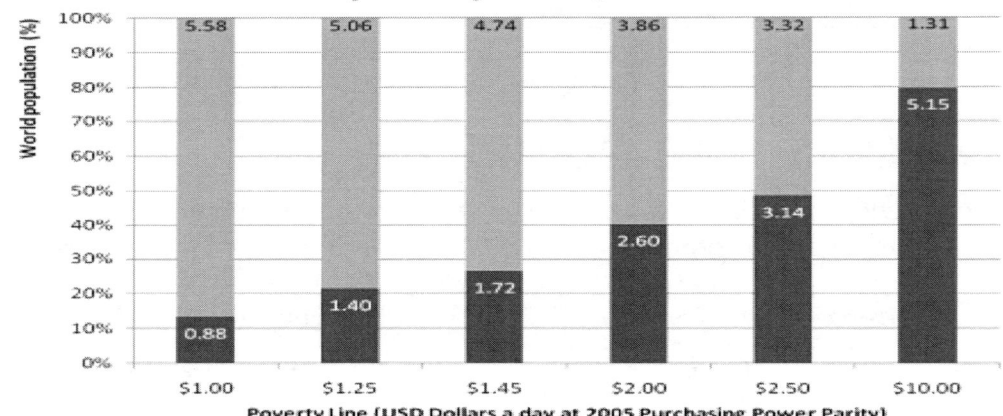

DATA

Percent of people in the world at different poverty levels, 2005

World population (%)

Poverty Line	Below	Above
$1.00	0.88	5.58
$1.25	1.40	5.06
$1.45	1.72	4.74
$2.00	2.60	3.86
$2.50	3.14	3.32
$10.00	5.15	1.31

Poverty Line (USD Dollars a day at 2005 Purchasing Power Parity)
Numbers inside bars are world population at that indicator, in billions

■ Below the poverty line   ■ Above the poverty line

Source: World Bank Development Indicators 2008

http://go.worldbank.org

Almost half the world—over 3 billion people—live on less than $2.50 a day.

Global Life Expectancy

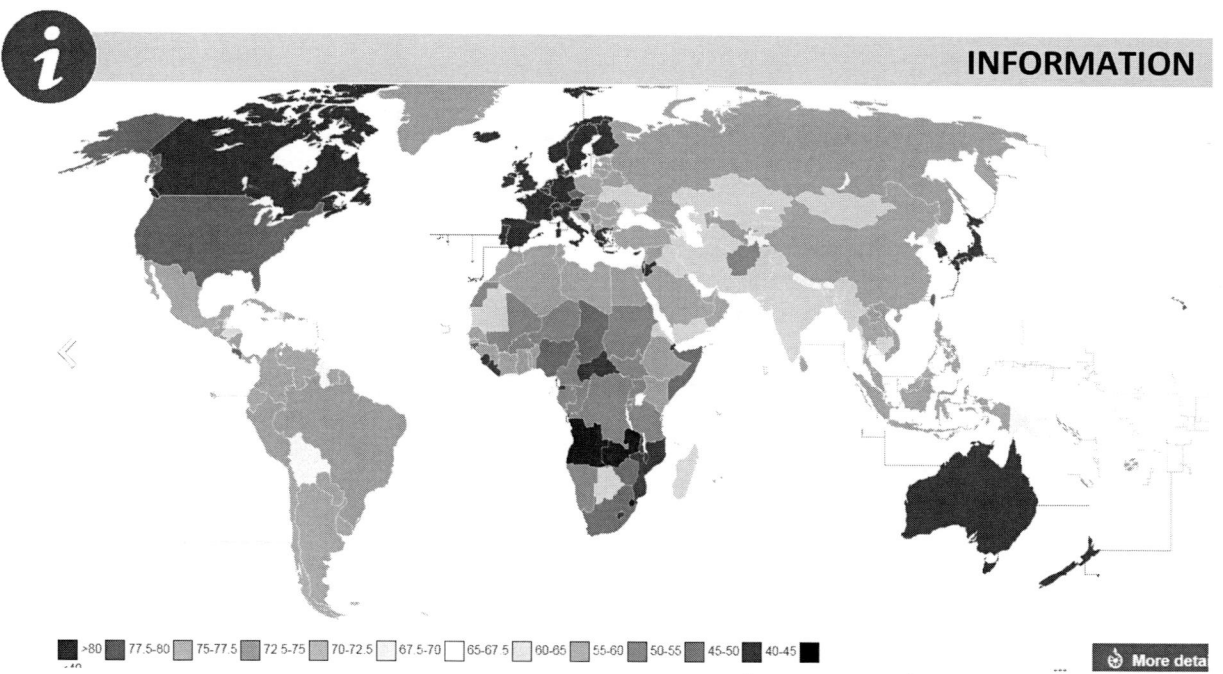

>80 ☐ 77.5-80 ☐ 75-77.5 ☐ 72.5-75 ☐ 70-72.5 ☐ 67.5-70 ☐ 65-67.5 ☐ 60-65 ☐ 55-60 ☐ 50-55 ☐ 45-50 ☐ 40-45 ☐

Life Expectancy 2015 Est. CIA World Factbook

Statistics

AVERAGE EARNINGS WORLDWIDE
The world's average income - total world income divided by total number of people - is about $7,000.

2007 The Globalist, theglobalist.com

NUMBER OF HUNGRY PEOPLE IN THE WORLD

http://www.worldhunger.org/articles/Learn/world%20hunger%20facts%202002.htm

REASONS FOR POVERTY

Many different factors have been cited to explain why poverty occurs. No single explanation has gained universal acceptance. Factors that have been alleged to cause poverty include:

✓ Overpopulation

✓ Global Distribution of Resources

✓ High Standards of Living and Costs of Living

✓ Inadequate Education and Employment

✓ Environmental Degradation

✓ Economic and Demographic Trends

✓ Individual Responsibility and Welfare

✓ Dependency

http://www.fightpoverty.mmbrico.com/poverty/reasons.html

BIBLICAL OBSERVATIONS ON POVERTY

    A. Poverty _____   Deut. 15:11, Matt 26:11, Mk 14:7, John 12:8

    B. Poverty may be a consequence of sinful personal _____ _____ (but not always)

                                                   Proverbs 10:4, 19:15

    C. Poverty may be a consequence of sinful choices _____ (but not always)

                                                        James 5:1-4

    D. Poverty is not _____ *Jesus was poor*   Matt 8:20, 2 Cor. 8:9

    E. God may have a _____ for the poor   James 2:5

BIBLICAL REASONS WHY CHRISTIANS SHOULD MINISTER TO THE POOR

    A. _____   Deut. 15:11; Lev 19:10; I John 3:17

    B. Paul's example   Galatians 2:10

    C. The principle of sowing and reaping   Galatians 6:7-10; Matthew 5:7

    D. God will _____ those who give   Proverbs 19:17, 22:9, 28:27

    E. When Christians give to the poor they are giving to _____ Matthew 25:31-46

A CHRISTIAN ATTITUDE TOWARD THE POOR

    A. Consider others better than ourselves   Philippians 2:3; I Cor 10:24

    B. We are not to be a respecter of persons   James 2:1-9

    C. We are to love our neighbor as ourselves   Matthew 22:39

    D. The Golden Rule   Matthew 7:12; Luke 6:31

    E. When you see a need, meet it if you can.   James 4:17' Luke 10 25-37

TEN PRINCIPLES: GIVING THROUGH AN ORGANIZATION

1. Accountability — Does the program demand accountability from the people it serves?
2. Character — Does the program stress the building of character? "Give a man a fish and feed him for a day. Teach him how to fish and feed him for a lifetime". (2 Thessalonians 3:10)
3. Discernment — Do the providers use judgment to give help on an individual basis?
4. Employment — Does the program require work of those who can work?
5. Freedom — Does the program teach recipients how to free themselves from their dependent status?
6. God — Does the program foster true self-esteem by leading them to their Creator and His principles?
7. Success Rate — Does the program have a success rate that can be quantified?
8. Assessment — Does the program conduct periodic assessment to determine its effectiveness?
9. Overhead — How much money donated goes directly to the poor?
10. Volunteers — Are volunteers utilized to keep cost down and to provide a meaningful ministry for people.

Programs that help the poor are intended to be a "_____" not a "_____".

TEN ACTIVITIES THAT CAN MAKE A DIFFERENCE

1. Volunteer at a soup kitchen

2. Open a food pantry and clothing center in the church

3. Tutor students and adults

4. Provide basic job training

5. Provide child care services for single parents or others who are in real need

6. Be a mentor to children from broken homes

7. Help with Habitat for Humanity

8. Work with urban shelters for the homeless

9. Clean up parks and recreational facilities to provide good activities for kids and families

10. Become informed about the specific needs of your community

How does a Biblical Worldview confront the Poverty Issue?

C_____ in that we are all _____

F_____ in that we are all _____

R_____ in that we are all _____

C_____ in that we are all _____

BIBLICAL WORLDVIEW AND CONTEMPORARY MORAL ISSUES RESOURCE LIST

Anderson, Kerby. Christian Ethics in Plain Language. Nashville: Thomas Nelson, 2005.

Beals, Art. Beyond Hunger: A Biblical Mandate for Social Responsibility. Portland, Oregon, Multnomah Press, 1985.

Bonevac, Daniel. Today's Moral Issues: Classic and Contemporary Perspectives. New York, New York: McGraw-Hill Companies, 2006.

Boss, Judith A. Analyzing Moral Issues. 2nd ed. Boston: McGraw-Hill Companies, 2002.

Boss, Judith A. Ethics for Life: A Text with Readings. Boston, McGraw-Hill Companies, 2004.

Clark, David K., and Robert V. Rakestraw. Readings in Christian Ethics: Issues and Applications. Vol. 2. Grand Rapids: Baker Books, 2000.

Clark, David K., and Robert V. Rakestraw. Readings in Christian Ethics: Theory and Method. Vol. 1. Grand Rapids: Baker Books, 2000.

Colson, Charles, and Nancy Pearcey. How Shall We Then Live. Wheaton: Tyndale House Publishers, 1999.

Evan, Tony. Let's Get To Know Each Other: What White and Black Christians Need to Know About Each Other. Nashville: Thomas Nelson Publishers, 1995.

Feinberg, John S. and Paul D. Ethics for a Brave New World. Wheaton, Illinois: Crossway Books, 2010.

Geisler, Norman L. Christian Ethics: Contemporary Issues and Options. Grand Rapids: Baker Books, 2010.

Gibbs, David. Fighting for Dear Life: The Untold Story of Terri Schiavo and What It Means for All of Us. Minneapolis, Minnesota: Bethany House, 2006.

Gordon, Wayne L. Real Hope in Chicago. Grand Rapids, Michigan: Zondervan Publishing House, 1995.

Green, Joel B., gen. ed. Dictionary of Scripture and Ethics. Grand Rapids, Michigan: Baker Academic, 2011.

Grudem, Wayne. Business for the Glory of God: The Bible's Teaching on the Moral Goodness of Business. Wheaton, Illinois: Crossway, 2003.

_____. Countering the Claims of Evangelical Feminism: Biblical Responses to the Key Questions. Colorado Springs, Colorado: Multnomah Publishers, 2006.

_____. Politics According to the Bible: A Comprehensive Resource for Understanding Modern Political Issues in Light of Scripture. Grand Rapids, Michigan: Zondervan, 2010.

Harris, Joshua. I Kissed Dating Goodbye. Sisters, Oregon: Multnomah Books, 1997.

Heimbach, Daniel R. True Sexual Morality: Recovering Biblical Standards for a Culture in Crisis. Wheaton, Illinois: Crossway Books, 2004.

Hogsett, Jim A. A Worker Need Not Be Ashamed: How to Live the Christian Life in the Workplace. 1st Books, 2004.

Hollinger, Dennis. Choosing the Good: Christian Ethics in a Complex World. Grand Rapids, Michigan: Baker Academic, 2002.

_____. The Meaning of Sex: Christian Ethics and the Moral Life. Grand Rapids, Michigan: Baker Academic, 2009.

Humphrey, Derek. Dying with Dignity: Understanding Euthanasia. New York: Carol Publishing Group, 1992.

Kilner John F. Why The Church Needs Bioethics: A Guide to Wise Engagement with Life's Challenges. Grand Rapids, Michigan: Zondervan, 2011.

Kostenberger, Andreas J. God, Marriage, and Family: Rebuilding the Biblical Foundation. Wheaton, Illinois: Crossway Books, 2004.

Lapin, Daniel. America's Real War. Sisters, Oregon: Multnomah Publishers, 1999.

Levine, Carol. Taking Sides: Clashing Views on Bioethical Issues. Dubuque, Iowa: McGraw-Hill Company, 2008.

Murray, John. Principles of Conduct: Aspects of Biblical Ethics. Grand Rapids, Michigan: William B. Eerdmans Publishing Company, 1957.

Pearcey, Nancy. Total Truth: Liberating Christianity from Its Cultural Captivity. Wheaton, Illinois: Crossway Books, 2004.

Piper, John. Bloodlines: Race, Cross, and the Christian. Wheaton, Illinois: Crossway, 2011.

Piper, John and Wayne Grudem, ed. Recovering Biblical Manhood and Womanhood: A Response to Evangelical Feminism. Wheaton, Illinois: Crossway Books, 1991, 2006.

Rae, Scott B. Moral Choices: An Introduction to Ethics. Grand Rapids, Michigan: Zondervan, 2009.

Satris, Stephen. Taking Sides: Clashing Views on Moral Issues. Dubuque, Iowa: McGraw-Hill Company, 2008.

Shapiro, Ben. Brainwashed: How Universities Indoctrinate America's Youth. Nashville: WND Books, 2004.

Swindoll, Charles R. Sanctity of Life The Inescapable Issue. Dallas: Word Publishing, 1990.

Talley, Jim A. and Bobbie Reed. Too Close Too Soon: Avoiding the Heartache of Premature Intimacy. Nashville: Thomas Nelson Publishers, 2002.

VanDrunen, David. Bioethics and the Christian Life: A Guide to Making Difficult Decisions. Wheaton, Illinois: Crossway, 2009.

Wilkens, Steve. Beyond Bumper Sticker Ethics. Downers Grove: Intervarsity Press, 1995.

Williams, Jarvis J. One New Man: The Cross and Racial Reconciliation in Pauline Theology. Nashville, Tennesse: B&H Academic, 2010.